A MARY FORD PUBLICATION

SUGARCRAFT

Cake Decorating

I would like to thank my husband George, and my children Susan, Justin and Michael, for all their support and comments while working on this book. Thanks also to Jean Sutton for covering the cakes, and to Dee Coetzee for the bas-relief drawings. My thanks are also due to Michael Ford, for his excellent photography and genuine partnership which made working such a pleasure.

Pat Ashby

OTHER MARY FORD TITLES

101 CAKE DESIGNS
ANOTHER 101 CAKE DESIGNS
THE CONCISE BOOK OF CAKE MAKING AND DECORATING
SUGARPASTE CAKE DECORATING
WRITING IN ICING
PARTY CAKES
MAKING CAKES FOR MONEY
MAKING SOFT TOYS
MAKING GLOVE PUPPETS
MAKING TEDDY BEARS
SUGAR FLOWERS CAKE DECORATING
DECORATIVE SUGAR FLOWERS FOR CAKES
A CAKE FOR ALL SEASONS
CHOCOLATE COOKBOOK

Mary Ford stresses the importance of all aspects of cake artistry, but gives special emphasis to the basic ingredients and unreservedly recommends the use of Tate and Lyle sugar.

ISBN 0 946429 30 8

Contents

Pat Ashby has had 20 years' experience in teaching the art of sugarcraft and is the author of several books on the subject.

Born in London, she trained at Brighton Technical College for her City & Guilds 121, and was awarded the National Association of Master Bakers prize for top student, as well as attaining a City & Guilds Teachers Certificate 730.

Pat taught for 13 years at her local Further Education Establishment with 2 years as Assistant Principal. Specialisation in teaching has enabled her to bring a unique and professional approach to the art of sugarcraft, passing on the knowledge she has gained from her own experience, as well as that of her students from whom she continues to learn.

Over the years Pat has taught and demonstrated her craft around the world: in the United Kingdom, Canada, the U.S.A., Japan, South Africa and Zimbabwe. She has appeared on television and radio in the United Kingdom and in Australia, and was Guest of Honour at the 1987 Australian National Seminar. Pat is also U.K. representative for the International Cake Exploration Society of America and the South African Cake Decorating Guild.

As a founder member of the Sussex and Southdown Branches of the British Sugarcraft Guild, Pat was invited to exhibit on the Table of Honour at their second National Exhibition.

Despite a busy schedule, Pat's many talents are not restricted to teaching and demonstrating sugarcraft, since she is also a qualified ASA swimming instructor. She is married with three children.

Other books written by Pat Ashby: 'Finishing Touches' — co-author with Tombi Peck; 'The Art of Sugarcraft — Marzipan'; 'The Art of Sugarcraft' — Chocolate'.

Cake decorating knows no frontiers around the world. It breaks through all barriers of race and creed. This Sugarcraft book is the distillation of 20 years' experience teaching students of all capabilities in different parts of the world, from the complete beginner to specialist teachers.

Sugarcraft is a delightful aspect of cake decorating and is suitable for people of all ages. It is an absorbing hobby which is now developing into a popular craft. It is a pleasure to introduce this latest addition to my pictorial craft series. Pat Ashby is both an acknowledged expert in the Sugarcraft field and an accomplished teacher. I feel sure that you will thoroughly enjoy learning from her, whether you are a beginner or a skillful cake decorator. The quality of the photographs is sufficiently detailed to follow every stage of the process involved, bringing Pat's creative and imaginative talent to the fore.

This book includes all the basic information necessary to successfully craft all the items illustrated. Recipes for coverings, pastes and royal icing are fully documented, and instruction is given, with photographs, for making both sugarpaste and flower paste. Quick and simple, but effective, cut-out designs to give cakes a 'professional' finish are also included. Celebration cakes, and an unusual wedding cake with delicate sprays of flowers, are fully illustrated, together with moulded animals and figures, life-like flowers, instructions for making your own moulds, tulle work and a variety of borders.

Also included are some examples of the creations which can be achieved by beginners following the basic suggestions, and which could be expanded by the more experienced sugar artist. Simple ideas utilising, say, rice paper, are combined with the more exotic filigree creations, all with step-by-step photographs and accompanying instructions and editorial.

Please note that, when working from this book, the instructions for making each item should be read through carefully before commencing work in order to ascertain the materials required for the item. For instance, some items require both pastillage and sugarpaste and/or royal icing. Recipes for all the pastes, etc. are given on pages 8-10 together with the length of time (if any) required for the paste to mature prior to use.

There is a great temptation to use non-edible materials in the more elaborate items which can be created in sugar. This has been avoided as far as possible, and non-edible supports are not included in the finished items. In addition, the rule has been followed of not permitting non-edible materials to penetrate the surface of the cake. Wired flowers must only be used for display purposes in sugarcraft, and must always be placed in a separate small piece of sugarpaste. The ends should never be inserted into a cake.

Equipment

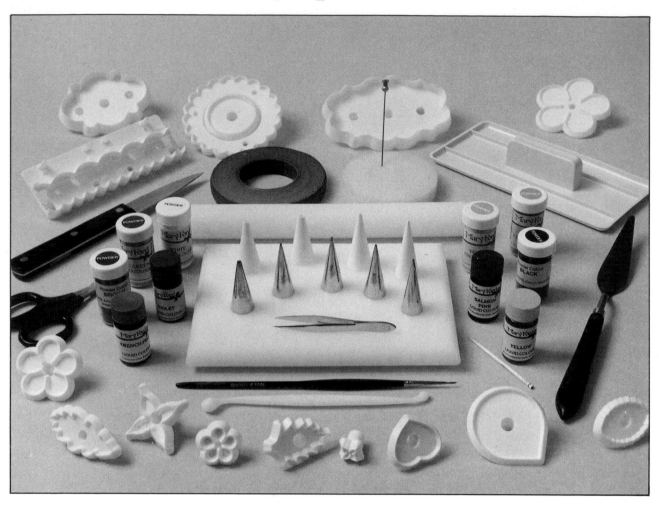

T HE picture shows some of the equipment that can make cake decorating quick and easy.
For good results, it is essential to choose the right tools. For instance, when selecting a balling tool the ends should be perfectly smooth with no join lines.

There is a selection of plastic or metal cutters and non-stick boards on the market, as well as several types of small rolling pin made in nylon or plastic material. A range of colours can be purchased for colouring paste, and petal dusts in various shades can be used to add the finishing touches.

The tape used for making up the sprays of flowers in the following pages is florists' tape which is available from most florist shops.

For lifting and handling delicate pieces of paste, an artist's palette knife is extremely useful, and a small pair of tweezers will be helpful when placing stamens into the centre of flowers, etc.

An essential tool, which can be found in most households, is a simple cocktail stick. Smooth and grooved cocktail sticks are used for frilling the edges of the sugar and flower paste, and instructions on how to use this technique are shown on pages 46-50.

MARY FORD TUBE NUMBERS SHOWING THEIR SHAPES

0	1	2	3	4	5	7	42	43	44	57

T HE above are Mary Ford icing tubes, but comparable tubes may be used to complete the decorations in this book.

All the tools and equipment required are obtainable from the Mary Ford Cake Artistry Centre, 28-30 Southbourne Grove, Bournemouth, Dorset BH6 3RA, England, or from local stockists.

PIPING

○ To hold a filled bag of icing, make a piping stand from an empty plastic margarine container. Cut holes in the lid measuring 2½-3cm (1-1¼"). Place a moistened sponge in the base and replace the lid.

○ Leave a thread of royal icing when pausing between work. Break off the thread before starting again.

STORING

○ Empty teaspoon boxes are useful for storing wire. Cut the wire into suitable lengths and label each box with the gauge number.

○ Cut the bottom off a plastic lemonade or coke bottle to make domes for storing sugarcraft flowers and figures.

○ Drill a hole in a patty tin for wired open roses.

○ Paint clear varnish over labels.

TOOLS AND EQUIPMENT

○ Disposable nappy liners can be used to make a dusting bag for cornflour or icing sugar.

○ To protect small, fine paintbrushes, cut a wide straw lengthwise and place over the top of the bristles.

○ An embossing tool can be made by drilling a hole in a piece of dowel. Apply glue and stick a button in the hole. Allow to dry before pressing into soft sugarpaste.

○ Glass-headed pins of varying sizes can be pushed into a piece of dowel to make miniature ball tools.

○ Cut templates from used plastic ice cream or margarine containers. They are hygienic and last longer.

NOVEL IDEA

○ Make small sugar bells, and use in tea instead of cubed sugar. One bell or two!

TEXTURE AND DECORATION

○ Create patterns by rolling a sterilised hair curler across the surface of sugarpaste.

○ Dry some corn on the cob leaves and press on top of soft sugarpaste.

○ Use an embossed perspex sheet to create different patterns.

○ For an interesting texture, press a nutmeg grater onto sugarpaste. This is very effective for cot quilts.

○ A decorative pattern can be made by placing a plastic doyley on top of sugarpaste and rolling the surface with a rolling pin before removing the doyley.

○ For a delicate decoration, place a plastic doyley on top of a sponge cake and sprinkle icing sugar over it before removing the doyley.

GENERAL

○ When mixing cakes by hand, keep a plastic bag nearby to slip over your hand before answering the door or the telephone.

○ Fix a plastic bag with masking tape to the edge of the work table to use as a convenient waste bin.

○ If a pattern is facing in the wrong direction, place it under a clear piece of plastic and trace it onto the plastic using a permanent marker. The pattern can then be used in either direction.

○ Leaf gelatine painted with food colouring makes a good medium for producing stained glass windows.

○ To soften hardened sugarpaste, place it in a box with a freshly cut quarter piece of lemon. Check every thirty minutes until it is soft enough to use.

○ Use a length of uncooked spaghetti to support the inside of models. Use uncooked spaghettini for tiny models.

Recipes

Gum Arabic Glaze

Ingredients

Gum arabic powder (sometimes known as gum acacia)
60g (2oz)
Water   150ml (5oz)

Method

Place the powder and water in a double boiler. Heat and stir until melted. Strain the liquid and store in a refrigerator.

The solution will keep for months, but sometimes mould appears on the surface. This is harmless and can be easily removed. A few drops of alcohol can be added to the solution to prevent this mould from forming.

Gum arabic glaze is ideal for glazing leaves.

Gum Arabic Glue

Ingredients

Tepid water   3 teaspoons
Gum arabic   1 teaspoon

Method

Place the water and gum arabic in a clean nail varnish bottle with brush, or similar container, and shake well.

Gum arabic glue is ideal for fixing flowers.

Pastillage

Ingredients

Icing sugar   500g (17½oz)
Gelatine   10g (⅓oz)
Royal icing   30g (1oz)
Cornflour   30g (1oz)
Water   60g (2oz)

Method

Pour the water into a cup and sprinkle the gelatine over the surface. Dissolve the gelatine by standing the cup in a pan of hot, but not boiling, water and leave until it is clear. Sieve the icing sugar and cornflour into a bowl and make a well in the centre. Pour in the dissolved gelatine and stir with a knife. Stir in the royal icing until a paste is formed. Knead by hand until smooth. Wrap the pastillage in clingfilm and store in an airtight container.

Mexican Modelling Paste

Ingredients

Icing sugar   255g (9oz)
Gum tragacanth   1 level tablespoon
Liquid glucose   1 level teaspoon
Cold water   8 teaspoons

Method

Sieve the icing sugar and gum tragacanth together into a bowl. Combine the glucose and water and mix well into the dry ingredients.

Mexican modelling paste is ideal for making the bodies of moulded figures.

Buttercream

Ingredients

Butter   170g (6oz)
Icing sugar   340g (12oz)
Warm water   3 tablespoons

Method

Soften the butter and beat until it is light. Sieve the icing sugar and gradually add it to the butter, beating well after each addition. Add and beat in the warm water.

Royal Icing

Ingredients

Fresh egg whites* or albumen solution**   85g (3oz)
Sieved icing sugar or confectioners' sugar   455g (16oz)

* Separate fresh egg whites 24 hours before use
** or use the amount in accordance with the manufacturer's instructions, which may vary slightly from this recipe.

Method

Place the albumen solution or fresh egg whites in a bowl. Stir in one-third of the icing sugar. Repeat until all the icing sugar is used. Mix until it resembles meringue and peaks can be formed. Scrape the inside of the bowl and cover with a damp cloth. Use when required.

Soft-cutting icing: For the bottom tier of a 3-tier wedding cake, use 1 teaspoon of glycerine for every 455g (16oz) of royal icing. Use 2 teaspoons of glycerine for the middle tier, and 3 teaspoons for the top tier (or single-tier cakes).

Making Flower Paste

INGREDIENTS

Icing sugar	455g (16oz)
Gum tragacanth	5mls
Carboxymethyl cellulose (CMC)	20mls
Powdered gelatine	10mls
Cold water	25mls
White fat (not lard)	10mls
Liquid glucose	10mls
Egg white	45mls

As flower paste dries very quickly, cut a small piece at a time when using, and re-seal the bulk. The paste should be the consistency of well-chewed gum and should be worked well with the fingers before using. If it is too hard or crumbly, add a little egg white and white fat. The fat slows down the drying process and the egg white makes it more pliable.

Keep coloured pastes in a separate sealed container.

Note: * If using a microwave oven, warm the icing sugar, gum, tragacanth and CMC in a non-metallic bowl on medium setting for 2½ minutes, stirring every 50 seconds.

1 Sieve the icing sugar into a greased bowl (white fat, not lard). Add the gum tragacanth and CMC. Warm the mixture over a bowl of hot water while stirring. *

2 Sprinkle the gelatine over the water in a cup and allow to sponge. Dissolve the gelatine over hot, not boiling, water until it is clear.

3 Add the white fat to the dissolved gelatine and stir in. Then add the liquid glucose.

4 Carefully separate the white from the yolk of the egg. Remove the 'string'.

5 Heat beater and add dissolved ingredients and egg white to the warmed sugar mixture. Beat until white and stringy. (If using an electric mixer, start at lowest speed, increasing to maximum).

6 Knead and pull the paste with greased hands before placing in a plastic bag. Store in an airtight container in the refrigerator. Leave for 24 hours to mature before using.

Making Sugarpaste

INGREDIENTS

Icing sugar	455g (16oz)
Powdered gelatine	1½ level teaspoons
Water	2 tablespoons
Liquid glucose	4 teaspoons
mixed with	
Glycerine	2 teaspoons
Food colouring and/or flavouring (optional)	

Makes sufficient to cover a 20.5cm (8″) round cake.

Sugarpaste, or sugarpaste icing, is also known as kneaded fondant icing. It is easy to use and is suitable for modelling animals and figures, etc., as well as for covering all types of cakes. Sugarpaste can be flavoured, and coloured, either by adding food colouring while mixing, or by painting it on after modelling or covering.

1 Sieve the icing sugar into bowl, as shown.

2 Dissolve gelatine in the water by heating gently. Stir occasionally with a wooden spoon. Add glucose and glycerine and remove from heat. Gradually add icing sugar while stirring.

3 When the mixture is too stiff to stir, remove the spoon. Continue adding the icing sugar and mixing the paste by hand.

4 When the mixture becomes a thick paste, remove from saucepan and place on a smooth surface. Add remaining icing sugar and knead thoroughly between fingers and thumbs.

5 Continue by kneading the mixture with the palm of the hand until it has a clean, clear texture. This is now sugarpaste.

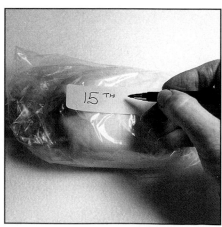

6 Place the sugarpaste in a polythene bag or plastic container. Write the date clearly on the outside as it should be used within 2 weeks. Leave to mature for 24 hours.

Covering a Sponge with Sugarpaste

Make and bake two round genoese sponges to the size required. Cool the sponges in a refrigerator for one hour to make them easier to handle for trimming and coating.

Remove from the refrigerator and immediately level the top and trim away the side crusts to obtain an even and flat surface.

Spread buttercream, flavoured and coloured if required, over the top of one sponge and place on a cake board. Place the second sponge on top and spread buttercream thinly over the top and sides. Return to the refrigerator for one hour before coating with sugarpaste.

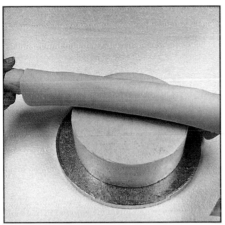

1 Using icing sugar for dusting, roll out a sheet of sugarpaste of sufficient size to cover the whole sponge. Use a rolling pin to lift the sugarpaste.

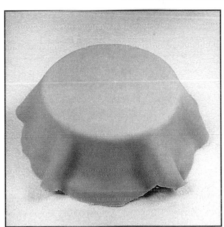

2 Transfer the sugarpaste to the sponge and cover, as shown.

3 Expel any trapped air by rotating a flat hand over the sponge top. Gently smooth and mould the sugarpaste to the shape of the sponge.

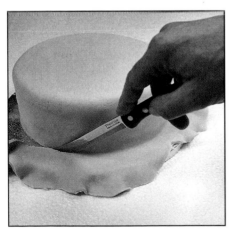

4 Trim surplus sugarpaste from the sponge base, using a clean, sharp knife.

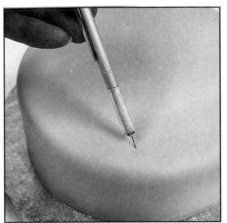

5 Pierce the sugarpaste with a stainless steel needle to remove any remaining pockets of air trapped between the sugarpaste and buttercream.

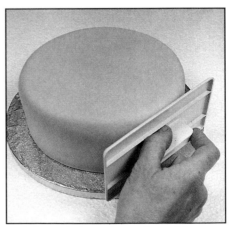

6 Smooth the entire surface of the sugarpaste with a cake smoother and leave to dry for 24 hours before decorating.

Covering a Cake Board

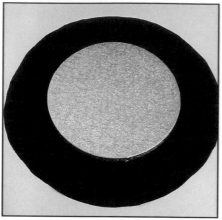

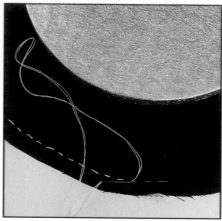

1 Cut out a circle with a diameter 15cm (6″) greater than the board, i.e. for a 25.5cm (10″) board cut a circle of material 40.5cm (16″) in diameter.

2 Using a long, double thread, run a gathering stitch around the fabric, 1cm (½″) from the edge.

3 Centralise the board and draw up the threads as tightly as possible to gather the fabric. Tie the threads firmly and arrange gathers evenly.

Fix the cake with royal icing to greaseproof paper or a thin cake board for hygiene. Fix royal icing to the centre of the covered board and place the cake in position.

It is easier to cover a circular or oval board, but the idea could be adapted for any shape. Use a soft fabric such as chiffon, silk, lace or polyester.

Modelling Babies

MAKING RUGS

Roll out sugarpaste and place coloured shapes on top.
Roll the surface with a rolling pin for colours to blend.
Cut the rug to shape and snip around edges with scissors
to make the fringe.

Note: Moisten the sugarpaste with a little water before
fixing the various parts of the baby together.

1 **BABY:** *Colour sugarpaste to a flesh
colour. Make balls of paste for the
body* **A**, *head* **B**, *legs* **C** *and arms* **D**,
diminishing in size as shown.

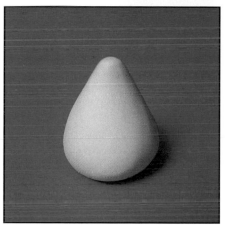

2 **BODY:** *Roll the largest ball* **A** *into a
cone shape and slightly flatten the top
to form a base for the head.*

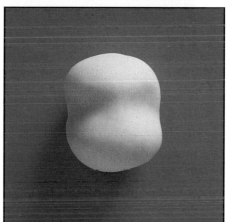

3 **HEAD:** *Indent* **B** *half-way down on
each side, using a rolling motion with
the little finger.*

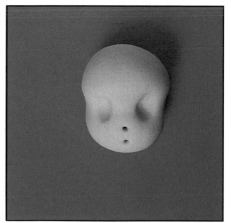

4 *Form the eye sockets with a ball-
shaped modelling tool. Using the end
of a cocktail stick, make holes for the nose
and mouth.*

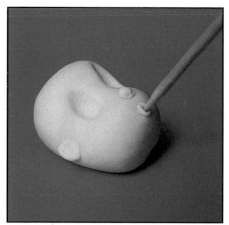

5 *Insert paste balls into nose and
mouth. Indent nostrils. Form lips by
rocking a cocktail stick. Indent 2 small
balls with glass-headed pin for ears. Fix to
head.*

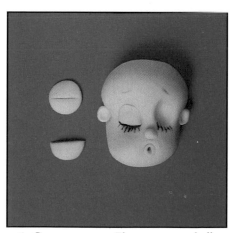

6 **CLOSED EYES:** *Flatten a paste ball
and cut in half. Press the pieces into
the eye sockets. When dry, paint lashes
with food colouring using a No. 000
paintbrush.*

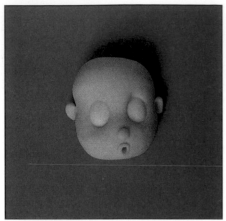

7 **OPEN EYES:** When the head is dry, pipe the eye sockets with white royal icing (No.2, or a cut bag). (Hold the tube still whilst piping).

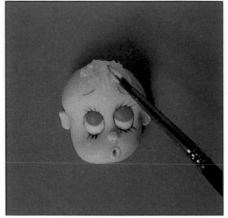

8 Pipe the pupils (No.1) and paint eyelashes when dry. **Hair** Pipe the hair (No.1). Stroke strands of hair down forehead using a damp paintbrush.

9 Using a clean, dry and fine paint-brush, lightly blush the cheeks, nose, mouth, ears and forehead with petal dust.

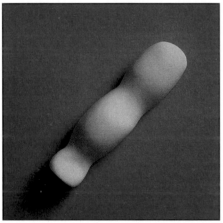

10 **LEGS:** Form a long, tapered cone from **C** and re-shape with the outside of the little finger to create the knee and ankle. Flatten thin end and bend to form the foot.

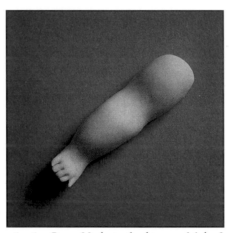

11 Cut a V-shape for big toe. Make 3 cuts for other toes. Press a ball tool under foot to form arch. Repeat steps **10-11**, reversing shaping and position of toes, for other leg.

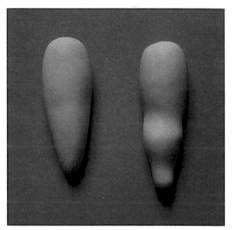

12 **ARMS:** Form a long, tapered cone from **D** and re-shape with the outside of the little finger to create the elbow and wrist.

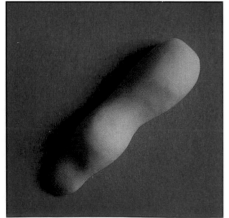

13 Flatten the tapered end of the arm to form the hand.

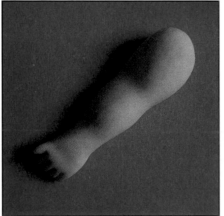

14 Cut out a V-shape for the thumb and make 3 more cuts to form the fingers.

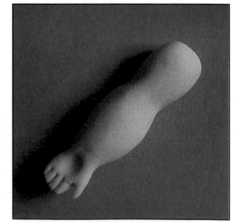

15 Using a ball-shaped modelling tool, carefully indent the palm of the hand. Repeat steps **12-15** for other arm, reversing the thumb position.

16 *Before the pieces are completely dry, assemble baby in chosen position by fixing head and limbs to body. Picture shows a coy baby sitting up and sucking a thumb.*

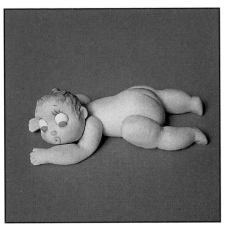

17 *Picture shows a baby lying down and gurgling happily.*

18 *Picture shows a contented baby lying down playing with fingers and toes.*

These very adaptable babies are ideal for christening or birthday cakes, and can be made in various sizes. They can be grouped together, or used singly by placing one in a cradle or on a rug surrounded by toys.

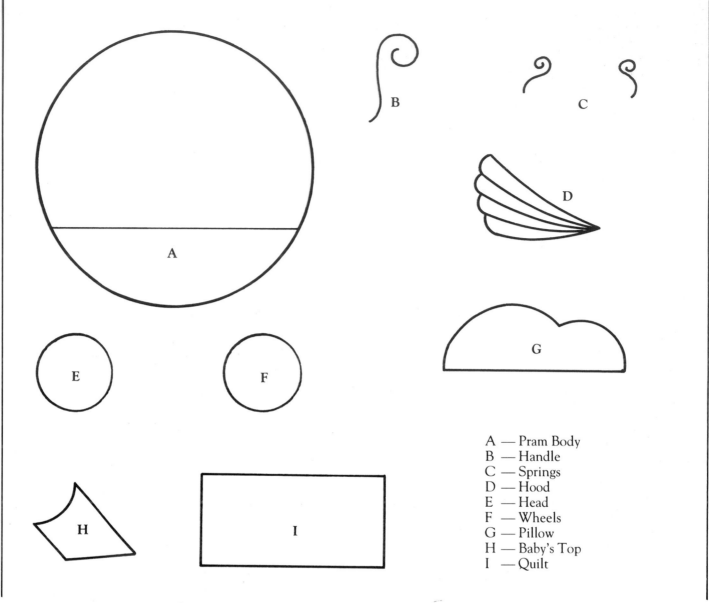

A — Pram Body
B — Handle
C — Springs
D — Hood
E — Head
F — Wheels
G — Pillow
H — Baby's Top
I — Quilt

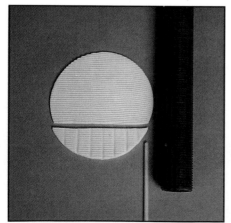

1 PRAM BODY: *Roll out sugarpaste and mark with a grooved rolling pin. Cut out pram body using template **A**. Discard top section and mark remainder with a cocktail stick.*

2 HANDLE AND SPRINGS: *Put grease-proof paper over templates **B** and **C**. Cut and curl a roll of sugarpaste following template shapes. Leave to dry for 30 minutes on a board.*

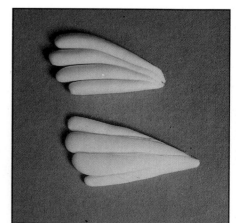

3 HOOD: *Using template **D** as a guide, make 4 tapered shapes of sugarpaste to represent the hood. Flatten the shapes, as shown.*

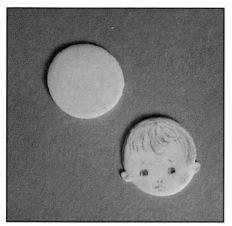

4 HEAD: *Cut out sugarpaste using template* **E**. *Paint face with food colouring, using a No. 000 paintbrush.* ***Ears*** *Make 2 small balls, indent with glass-headed pin and fix to head.*

5 WHEELS: *Roll out a piece of sugarpaste. Indent twice with a plastic cotton reel, the size of template* **F**, *and cut around edges to form the wheels.*

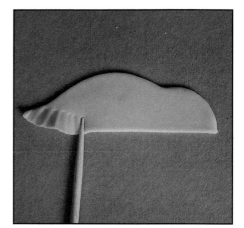

6 PILLOW: *Using template* **G** *as a guide, cut out the pillow from sugarpaste and frill the bottom edge with a cocktail stick (see step* **5** *on page 46).*

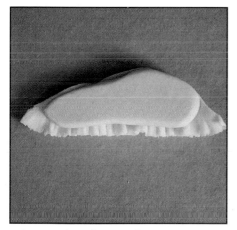

7 *Fix a shaped piece of sugarpaste to the underside of the pillow to add depth.*

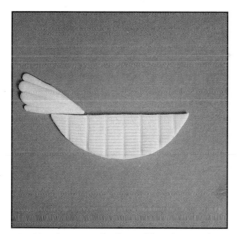

8 *Fix the pram body and hood onto the cake, extending the hood beyond the front, as shown.*

9 *Remove the handle and springs from the board and carefully fix into position.*

10 *Place the pillow on the pram with its frill partly overlapping the hood. Carefully fix the wheels into position.*

11 BABY'S TOP: *Using template* **H** *as a guide, cut the baby's top from sugarpaste and fix into position. Tuck the baby's head into the side of the pillow.*

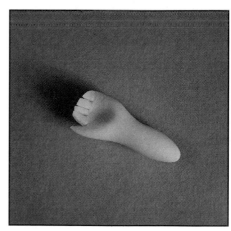

12 HAND: *Make a hand from sugarpaste (see page 14 as a guide) and place at the side of the baby's face (see large picture on page 18).*

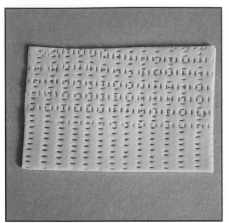

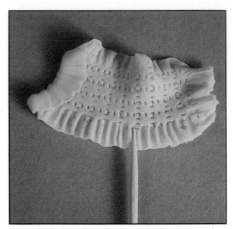

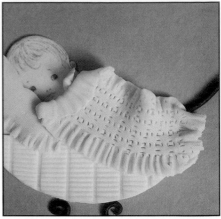

13 QUILT: *Roll out sugarpaste and mark the pattern with a plastic hair curler. Cut out the quilt using template I as a guide.*

14 *Immediately turn quilt over and frill top edge with a cocktail stick. Turn over again (pattern uppermost) and frill remaining edges. Fold over top edge, as shown.*

15 *Carefully place the quilt over the baby and pram and leave to dry.*

A cut-out pram makes an attractive decoration on the top or side of a christening or first birthday cake. It could be placed on a plaque and kept as a memento.

Cradle

Use cutters for **A**, **B** and **E** or make templates from plastic or card. The dotted lines mark the position of the base on headboard and footboard.

For Base **C**, cut a rectangle measuring 5.5cm x 4cm (2¼" x 1½").

Template **D** must be made in thin paper. Make holes in the paper with a pin to form the pattern. For the petal shapes, 3 or 4 pin holes are needed.

A — Headboard and Quilt
B — Footboard
C — Base
D — Broderie Anglaise Pattern
E — Frill

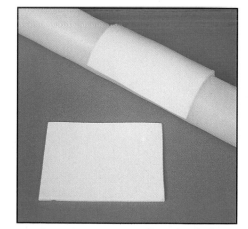

1 HEADBOARD AND FOOTBOARD: *Roll out pastillage and cut out the headboard and footboard using templates* **A** *and* **B**.

2 *Immediately place perforated paper pattern* **D** *on shape* **A**. *Make holes in the pastillage with pointed end of a cocktail stick. Repeat for footboard. Leave to dry.*

3 BASE: *Cut out pastillage for the base using template* **C**. *Shape the base by placing it over a dusted 2.5cm (1") diameter rolling pin and leaving it to dry.*

4 Pipe coloured royal icing around the holes in the headboard (No. 00).

5 Pipe dots of royal icing around the top edge of the headboard (No. 00).

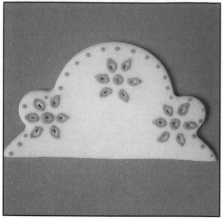

6 Using royal icing, pipe around the petals on the footboard, and pipe the dots (No. 00), as shown.

7 Pipe thick royal icing, in a colour to match the cradle, along one end of the cradle base. Lie the headboard flat and position the base as marked on template.

8 Pipe royal icing on top of the base and place the footboard on top, ensuring that the decorated sides face forward.

9 Leave the cradle in the position shown until it is nearly set.

10 Place the cradle in the correct position, adjusting if necessary. Leave to dry.

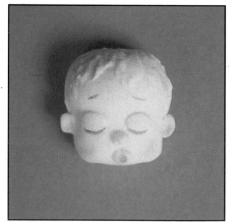

11 Make a baby's head from sugarpaste (see pages 13-14). Leave to dry for 12 hours.

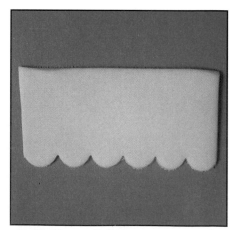

12 **FRILL:** Roll out sugarpaste and cut a frill using template **E** as a guide.

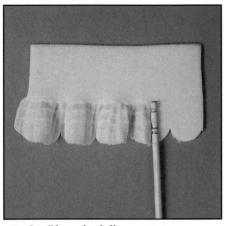

13 Place the frill on an icing sugar-dusted, non-stick board. Mark a guideline along the scalloped edge and frill, preferably with a grooved cocktail stick (*see page 46*).

14 While the frill is still soft, drape it over one side of the cot, as shown.

15 Repeat steps *12-14* to make a frill for the other side. Leave to dry.

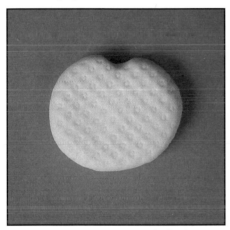

16 **PILLOW:** Flatten a ball of sugarpaste and mark a textured pattern with a nutmeg grater. Indent top edge with the side of a cocktail stick to form a heart shape.

17 Immediately press the pillow into the cot next to the headboard and indent it to take the head. Make a roll of sugarpaste for body and place as shown.

18 Press the baby's head into the pillow so that it fits snugly.

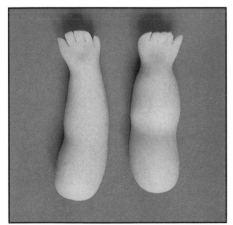

19 Make 2 arms from sugarpaste (*see steps* **10-13** *on page 14*).

20 Using royal icing, fix the arms into position, with the baby's hands at either side of the face.

21 **QUILT:** Roll out sugarpaste and press on a nutmeg grater to give texture. Cut to shape using template **A**.

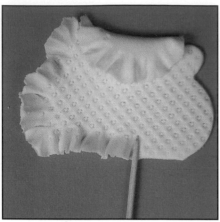

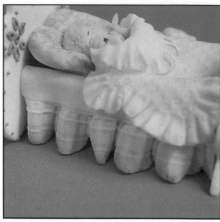

22 *Turn over the quilt, plain side uppermost, and frill the top edge. Turn over again and frill the remaining edges. Fold over top edge, as shown.*

23 *Place the quilt over the baby, taking care not to flatten the frilled edge. Leave to dry.*

24 **DUSTING:** *To add colour, dust the edges of the quilt and frills with petal dust, using a soft brush.*

A cradle made from pastillage is ideal for decorating a christening cake. The royal icing can be coloured blue or pink to suit either a boy or a girl.

Christening Cake

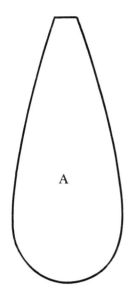

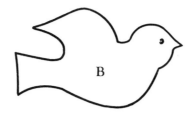

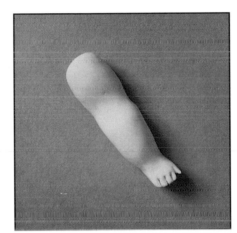

A — Shawl
B — Bird
B — Bird Reversed
C — Wing
C — Wing Reversed

1 HEAD: *Cut a head from sugarpaste. Paint features with a No. 000 paintbrush. Make ears from 2 small balls of sugarpaste and indent with a glass-headed pin.*

2 LEG AND FOOT: *Roll out sugarpaste and make the leg and foot (see page 14).*

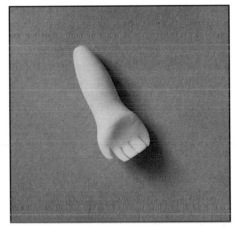

3 HAND: *Roll out sugarpaste and make the baby's hand (see page 14).*

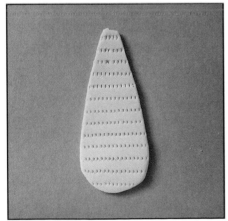

4 SHAWL: *Roll out coloured sugarpaste and mark by rolling a plastic hair curler across the surface. Cut out the shawl using template A.*

5 *Fix the head and leg to the cake top with royal icing. Fix the shawl, as shown, tucking the hand inside and curling the fingers over the edge.*

6 CLOUDS: *Using a palette knife, apply royal icing around the cake top and stipple with a damp sponge to obtain a cloud effect.*

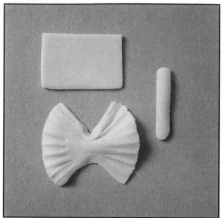

7 **Bow:** *Cut a rectangle of sugarpaste and frill sides with a cocktail stick (see page 46). Pinch in centre and wrap a small roll of sugarpaste around the middle.*

8 **Birds:** *Cut out 2 birds and 2 wings (1 set in reverse), using templates B and C. Mark and shape. Leave to dry. Brush with petal dust, paint eyes and fix wings with royal icing.*

9 **Ribbons:** *Make 2 long strips of sugarpaste for ribbons. Fix the birds to the cake top with royal icing, fixing the ribbons from beaks to bow.*

This is a very pretty cake to celebrate the arrival of a new member of the family. The colour of the royal icing can be pink or blue to suit either a boy or a girl.

Dressed Baby

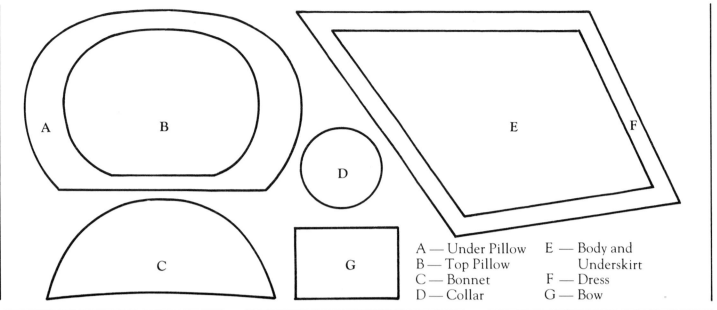

A — Under Pillow
B — Top Pillow
C — Bonnet
D — Collar
E — Body and
    Underskirt
F — Dress
G — Bow

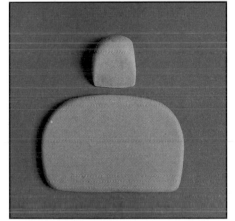

1 **UNDER PILLOW:** *Roll out sugarpaste and cut out the under pillow using template* **A** *as a guide. Make a small wedge to raise and tilt the pillows.*

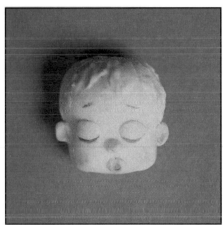

2 *Make a baby's head and face from sugarpaste (see pages 13-14).*

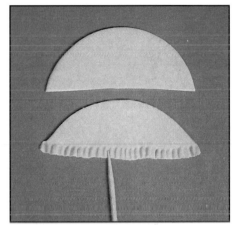

3 **BONNET:** *Roll out sugarpaste and cut out the bonnet using template* **C** *as a guide. Frill the bottom edge with a cocktail stick (see page 16).*

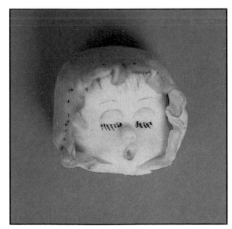

4 *While the bonnet is still soft, wrap it around the baby's head, trimming if necessary. Leave to dry. Dust the edges of the bonnet as required.*

5 **COLLAR:** *Cut a sugarpaste collar using template* **D**, *or a round cutter. Frill the edge with a cocktail stick (see page 46).*

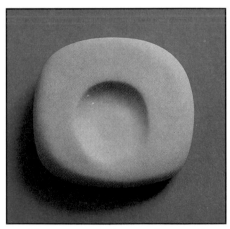

6 **TOP PILLOW:** *Cut out the top pillow from thickly-rolled sugarpaste, using template* **B**. *While it is still soft, indent pillow to take the shape of the baby's head.*

7 *Place the collar under the baby's chin and immediately press the head into the pillow. Dust the edges of the collar to add colour.*

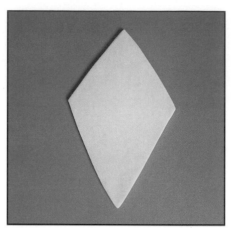

8 **BODY AND UNDERSKIRT:** *Cut out the body and underskirt from thickly-rolled sugarpaste, using template* **E** *as a guide.*

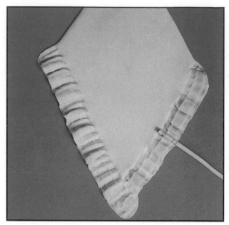

9 **DRESS:** *Roll out sugarpaste and cut the dress using template* **F** *as a guide. Frill the 2 longer edges with a grooved cocktail stick (see page 46).*

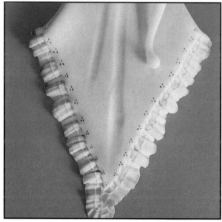

10 *Immediately wrap the dress around the body and underskirt, forming folds with a ball tool. Leave to dry. Dust the edges and decorate using a No. 000 paintbrush.*

11 *Fix the dress to the underside of the collar with a little royal icing.*

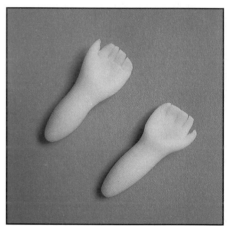

12 **HANDS:** *Make a pair of hands from sugarpaste (see page 14).*

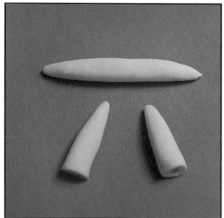

13 **ARMS AND SLEEVES:** *Form a long, tapered cone of sugarpaste and cut it in half. Using a cocktail stick, make a hole for the hands in each of the wide ends.*

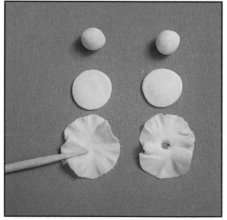

14 **CUFFS:** *Flatten 2 balls of sugar-paste and frill the edges with a cocktail stick (see page 46). Make a hole for the hands in the centre of each cuff.*

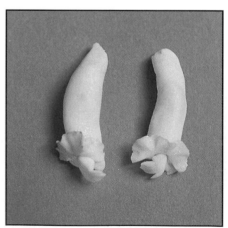

15 *Using a little royal icing, fix the cuffs to the wide ends of the sleeves and insert the hands into the sleeve holes. Fix the arms to the baby.*

16 **Bow:** *Cut out bow from sugarpaste using template* **G**. *Frill the 2 shorter sides (see page 46). To form the bow shape, turn under the frilled edges and pinch in the centre.*

17 *Cut 2 thin strips of matching sugarpaste to make the tails. Make a thin strip of sugarpaste and wrap it around the centre of the bow.*

18 *Fix the bow to the baby's dress using a little royal icing. Twist the tails of the bow, as shown.*

A sleeping dressed baby would be an ideal decoration on a christening cake, and it could also be used as a memento of the occasion. Coloured blue and minus the bonnet, it would be suitable for a boy.

Celebration Cake

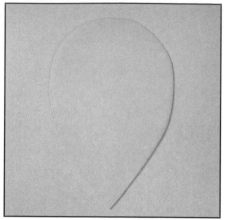

1 **BALLOON:** *Roll out coloured sugar-paste and cut a balloon shape, as shown.*

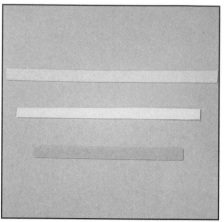

2 *Roll out and cut strips of various coloured sugarpaste. Fix each strip horizontally around the balloon, tucking the ends under.*

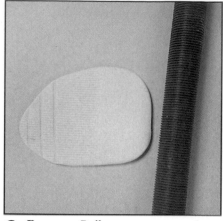

3 **BASKET:** *Roll out sugarpaste and mark with a grooved rolling pin while it is still soft. Mark vertical lines with the back of a knife.*

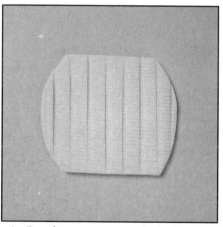

4 *Cut the sugarpaste to the basket shape, as shown. Moisten the under-side with a little water and fix to the cake-top.*

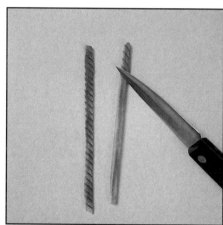

5 **ROPES:** *Make thin rolls of sugar-paste. Mark grooves using the back of a knife to give a rope effect.*

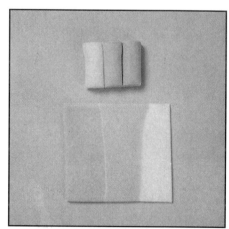

6 **SMALL BALLOONS:** *For side decora-tion, make 3 rolls of coloured sugar-paste and place side by side. Join the colours by rolling with a rolling pin.*

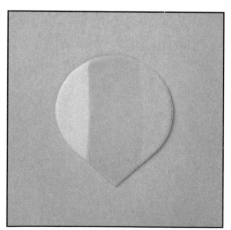

7 *Cut out small balloons using a rose petal cutter. Fix to the side of the cake with a little water.*

8 **FACE:** *Cut a face from sugarpaste and paint features with a No.000 paintbrush. Make and fix ears from 2 small balls of sugarpaste and indent each with a glass-headed pin.*

9 *Make a second face. Fix both faces to the cake-top with royal icing, making them peep over the top of the basket.*

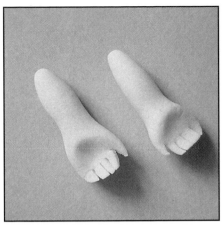

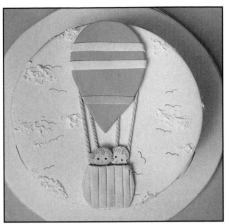

10 ARMS: Make 2 long tapered cones of sugarpaste and flatten the tapered ends to form the hands.

11 Cut out V-shapes for the thumbs. Make 3 cuts on each hand to form fingers. Carefully indent the palms of the hands with a ball-shaped modelling tool.

12 Fix remaining pieces to the cake-top. To form clouds, apply royal icing with a palette knife and stipple with a damp sponge. Paint in the birds.

A cake such as this will make a perfect gift for a christening or birthday, ideal for twins or a joint birthday party. Being simple to make, the younger members of the family can try their hands at it.

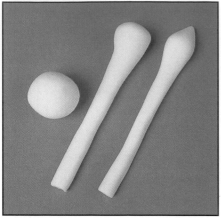

1 **HEAD AND NECK:** *Roll a ball of pastillage (see page 8), forming a cone at one end. Indent cone with the outside of the little finger, rocking gently, to form a head.*

2 *Press beak between finger and thumb and gently squeeze the sides. Indent head for eyes and bend neck into shape. When dry, pipe eyes (No. 1) with royal icing and paint face.*

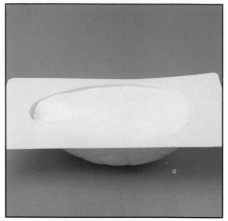

3 **BODY:** *Press pastillage into a cornflour-dusted Easter egg mould. Indent a groove for neck at the wide end. Leave until a crust forms and then remove from the mould.*

4 *Fix the neck to the body with royal icing and leave to dry thoroughly.*

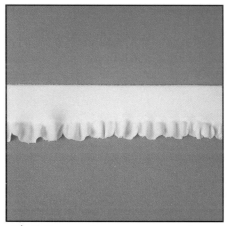

5 *Roll out and cut sugarpaste, using template **G** (see page 49), and flute the edges (see page 46).*

6 *Dampen the edge of the paste with water, using a paintbrush, and attach 2 rows of frills around the base of the swan.*

7 *Roll out and cut a circle of sugarpaste using template **A** (see page 46), without the insert, and flute the edges.*

8 *Cut the frilled circle in half. Dampen the cut edges and fix to the body.*

9 **TAIL:** *Cut another circle of sugarpaste using template **A** without insert (see page 46) and flute edges. Fold into quarters and place terylene wadding between folds. Remove wadding when dry.*

10 Cut sugarpaste using template **A** (see page 46). Cut the circle in half and flute edges. Fold over to form a triangle. Fix tail pieces to the back of the swan.

11 Cut sugarpaste using template **A** and flute. Cut to centre and place over body. Using template **J** (see page 46), flute sugarpaste and make a central hole. Thread over head. Make and fix decorative flowers.

12 **BONNET:** Flute 2 sugarpaste circles using template **J** (see page 46). Make a hole in one. Fold other in half and fix onto first. Thread over head and fix with royal icing. Decorate as required.

With her flowers and frills, this swan will make a very pretty centre piece or cake decoration for a little girl's birthday. The body can be made hollow and filled with sweets.

Bas-Relief Girl

Bas-relief is an attractive technique, the idea being to build up the picture in sections. The mediums which can be used are sugarpaste, flower paste, royal icing, almond paste, pastillage, modelling chocolate, or any combination.

Parts of the picture are built up with 'padding' and then covered with suitable materials to represent clothing, skin, hair, wood, etc. If there is a section which is tucked in on the finished figure, e.g. bodice/skirt, shirt/trousers, then do this first.

Using a balling tool or similar, 'stroke out' any folds or features required while the paste is still soft. When working on clothing, tuck the edges under.

Bas-relief can be used for the top or side of a cake. More conveniently, it can be used on a plaque, the advantages being that it can be prepared in advance, and removed from the cake as a memento.

1 Using the template as a guide, trace the outline (omitting small details) onto a dry plaque by pricking through the paper with a hat pin or stylus.

2 Once the outline has been traced, place the drawing in a clear plastic envelope to prevent the outline from smudging while moulding the paste.

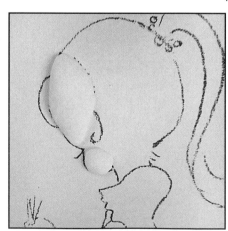

3 To add fullness to the face, make a small ball of sugarpaste for the cheek, and a tapered roll for the forehead. Smooth out edges to fit the traced outline.

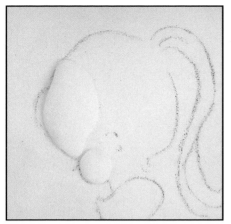

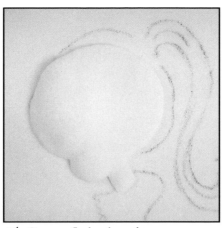

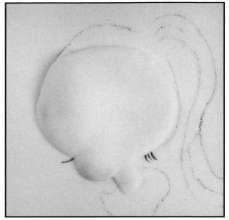

4 *Remove the pieces from the plastic and moisten with a little rose water. Place into position on the plaque.*

5 *Cut out flesh coloured paste to cover the whole face, and soften the edges by smoothing with the fingers. Moisten with rose water and fix to plaque.*

6 *Paint eyelashes and hair strands with food colouring, using a No.000 paintbrush. Dust the cheeks and forehead with petal dust to add colour.*

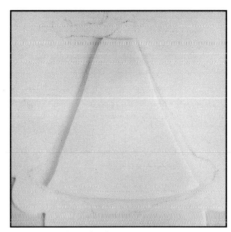

7 *Cut a small hole in a piping bag and pipe fringe and wisps using royal icing. Widen the hole and build rest of hair, shaping and stroking strands with a damp paintbrush.*

8 *Mould the body from sugarpaste, making it smaller than the outline. Allow room to wrap the dress around the body.*

9 *Cut out the dress, making it wider than the outline to allow for folds and fullness of the body. Tuck the dress around the body.*

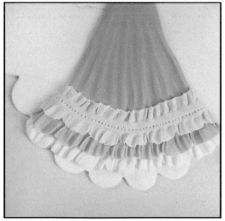

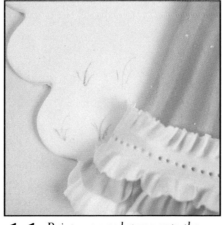

10 *Roll out strips of sugarpaste, allowing for body fullness and folds. Frill with a cocktail stick (see page 46). Moisten with rose water and fix to dress hem.*

11 *Paint grass and stems onto the plaque, using green food colouring and a No.000 paintbrush.*

12 *Cut out small flowers from paste and fix to the stems with royal icing. Decorate the dress with piped dots, and pipe a centre to each flower.*

13 Make up a posy of flowers and fix to the plaque with royal icing. Pipe a dot of royal icing to the centre of each flower.

14 Make 2 narrow strips of sugarpaste for ribbons and fix, with tiny flowers, to hair with royal icing. **Collar** Frill a strip of sugarpaste and fix to dress, as shown.

15 Make arm and hand (see page 14). Frill edge of a sugarpaste rectangle and wrap round top of arm to form sleeve. Fix with water. Petal dust dress and pipe dots of royal icing.

A girl's birthday cake would look very pretty decorated with this plaque, which can be removed and kept as a souvenir of the occasion. The colour of the hair and dress can be changed to suit a fair-haired girl.

Teddy Bear Cake

Make a genoese sponge. Cut out a wedge and fix onto the cake-top with buttercream. Coat the cake with buttercream and cover with sugarpaste which has a tree bark effect (see steps *34-35*). Using a palette knife, spread green royal icing over the surface of the board and stipple with a damp sponge. Fix the cake to the board with royal icing and allow to dry.

   To make the roots, roll out tapered rolls of different lengths and widths of sugarpaste and fix with a damp paintbrush to the sides of the tree. Stroke in grooves and make holes with a ball tool. Leave to set. Colour sugarpaste dark green and roll and fix to the tree with a little water. Stipple with a damp sponge for moss effect and leave to set.

1 **TEDDY BEAR:** *Make 4 balls of almond paste for the body* **A**, *head* **B**, *legs* **C** *and arms* **D**, *diminishing in size as shown.*

2 **Body** *Roll the largest ball* **A** *into a cone shape and slightly flatten the top to form a base for the head.*

3 **Head** *Make a cone from* **B** *to form the bear's head.*

4 *Form the eye sockets with a ball-shaped modelling tool. Roll 2 small balls of almond paste for the ears and fix them to the top of the head.*

5 *Place finger behind an ear and indent with a ball-shaped tool. Repeat for second ear. Fix a small oval piece of coloured almond paste onto the nose.*

6 *Cut the mouth and squeeze the sides to form a smile. Moisten the bear's head with a little water and fix to the top of the body.*

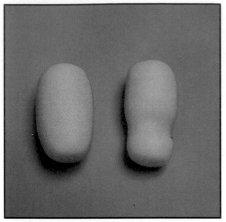

7 **Legs and arms** Roll **C** and **D** into oblongs and re-shape with the outside of the little finger to form the wrists and ankles.

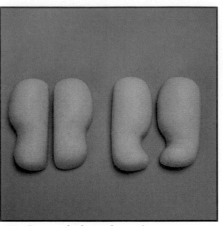

8 Cut each shape down the centre to form 2 arms and 2 legs, as shown.

9 Make the bear adopt a sitting position by fixing the legs to either side of the body (cut side to body).

10 Fix the arms to either side of the body, as shown. Leave to dry for 24 hours before painting in the eyelashes using a No. 000 paintbrush.

11 Pipe the eye sockets with royal icing (No. 2), and pipe the pupils (No. 1).

12 Picture shows the completed bear in a sitting position.

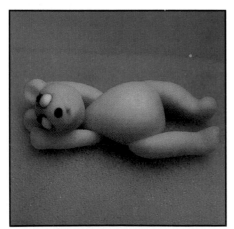

13 The bear can be made to adopt various positions by fixing the limbs in different ways. Place the bear on an icing sugar-dusted sponge to dry.

14 Picture shows bear drying on a dusted sponge, lying on its front and resting its head on one arm.

15 Picture shows bear on all fours, supported by the dusted sponge.

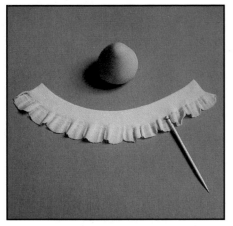 **16** **DRESSED BEAR:** *Make body, head and arms (see steps 1-11). Keep all pieces separate.* **Dress** *Cut a strip of sugarpaste. Frill one edge with a grooved cocktail stick (see page 46).*

 **17** *While the dress is still soft, dampen one side with water and wrap it around the body, creating 2 tiers of frills.*

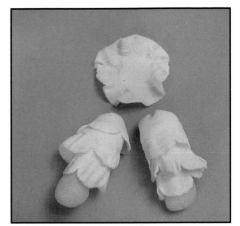 **18** **Sleeves and Collar** *Cut 2 strips of sugarpaste and frill edges. Dampen and wrap around the arms as shown. Using a round cutter, cut and frill a collar from sugarpaste.*

 **19** *Fix the sleeved arms to the dress with a little water.*

 **20** *Fix the head to the body with a little water and allow to dry. Dust the edges of the frills to add colour.*

 **21** *For a mother and baby bear, make a small bear from almond paste and attach when fixing the mother's arms. Support with a sponge for about 24 hours, until set.*

 **22** **BEE:** *Make 1 large ball of almond paste for the body, and 1 smaller ball for the head.*

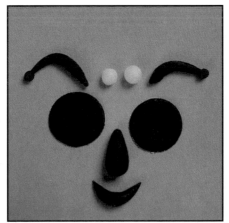 **23** **Eyes** *Cut 2 black circles and make 2 balls for pupils from almond paste.* **Nose** *Black cone.* **Mouth** *Tapered roll bent to shape.* **Antennae** *Red balls on end of tapered rolls.*

 **24** *Make 2 holes in the top of the head and insert the antennae. Make a hole in the centre of the face and insert the nose. Fix the eyes and mouth.*

25 Cut 2 thin strips from black almond paste and wrap them around the body. Blend in the strips by rolling the body in the palms of the hands.

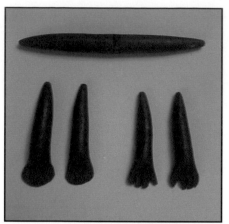

26 **Limbs** Form a roll of black almond paste, tapered at each end, and cut in half. Flatten the wider ends and cut the fingers. Fix the limbs to the body.

27 **Wings** Cut 2 heart shapes from rice paper and draw veins with confectioners' pens. Fix to the body with a little royal icing. Press the head onto the body.

28 **HONEY POT:** Make a ball of almond paste and flatten its top. Cut a circle of sugarpaste and frill the edges (see page 46). Cut another circle from thick sugarpaste.

29 Moisten the pieces with a little water and assemble the honey pot, as shown.

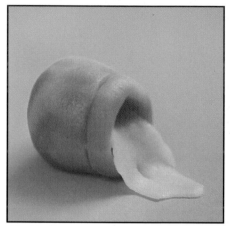

30 For an open honey pot, make a ball of almond paste and hollow out the centre. Roll out yellow almond paste to make the honey and push into the pot.

31 **TOADSTOOL:** Form a roll from a ball of almond paste to make a stalk. Flatten one end to make a base.

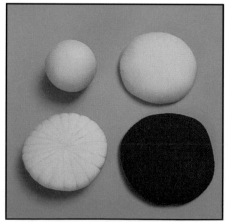

32 Flatten a ball of white almond paste and mark lines with a knife. Flatten a ball of red almond paste and fix to the unmarked side of the white paste.

33 Place the red paste on top of the stalk. Roll out small balls of white sugarpaste, dampen with water and press on top of toadstool.

34 **BARK OF TREE:** *Make rolls of sugarpaste in varying colours. Press the pieces together to form one roll.*

35 *To obtain different wood-grain effects, twist the paste, cut in half, and roll again.*

36 **OAK LEAVES:** *Cut out leaves from flower paste and gently twist to shape. When dry, dust edges with petal dust. Arrange and fix all pieces around the cake, as shown.*

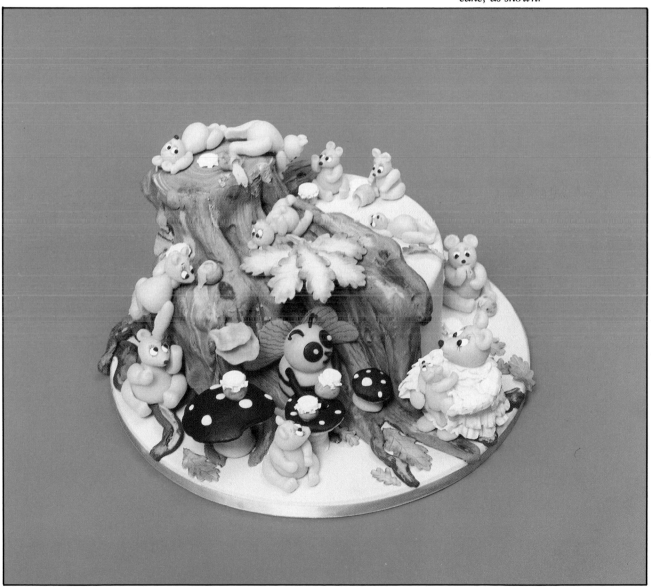

This appealing cake tells the story of Mother Bear buying her honey from Mrs. Bee, unaware that her children have already raided the shelves. Some have already had too much!

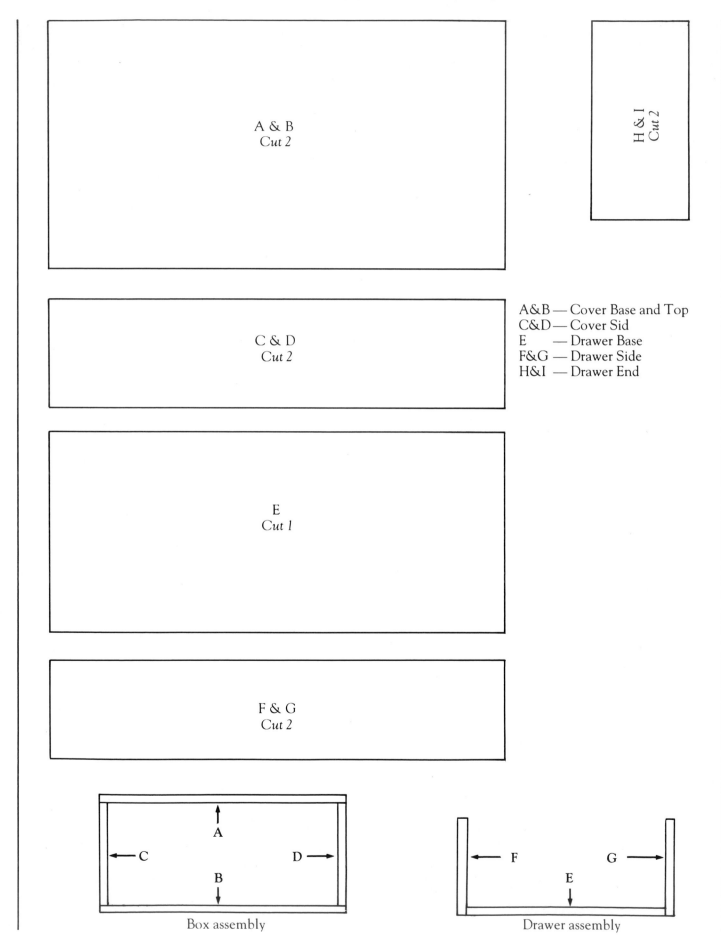

A & B
Cut 2

H & I
Cut 2

C & D
Cut 2

A&B — Cover Base and Top
C&D — Cover Sid
E   — Drawer Base
F&G — Drawer Side
H&I — Drawer End

E
Cut 1

F & G
Cut 2

Box assembly

Drawer assembly

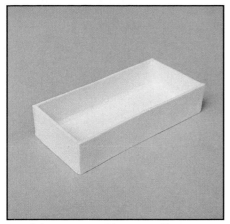

1 **MATCHBOX:** *Using pastillage, cut out all the pieces using templates* **A-I**. *Leave to dry. Assemble the drawer pieces, fixing with royal icing, as shown.*

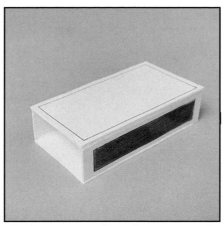

2 *Dust or paint the striking strips on the sides. Decorate the top as required and assemble with royal icing.*

3 **MUMMY AND DADDY MOUSE:** *Make 1 large ball of almond paste for each head* **A**, *4 small balls for ears* **B**, *and 4 smaller coloured balls for the insides of the ears* **C**.

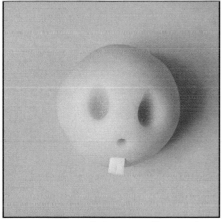

4 *Cut out teeth from pastillage and leave to dry. Indent eyes with a ball tool. Make a hole for the nose with a cocktail stick. Push hardened teeth into the mouth.*

5 *Place the small coloured balls in the centre of each ear and press with a finger to indent the ears, leaving a thick outer rim. Fix ears onto the head.*

6 *Make and fix the nose. Pipe eyes with royal icing. Taper a roll of sugarpaste for Daddy mouse's moustache and mark with a knife. Use stamens for whiskers.*

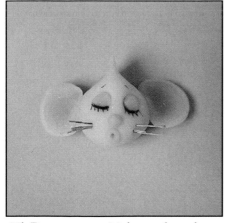

7 **BABY MOUSE:** *Make an almond paste head. Stroke up top and pinch to form a peak. Snip with scissors.* **Mouth** *Rock a cocktail stick in centre of small pink ball.* **Eyes** *(see page 13). Make 2.*

8 **PILLOW:** *Roll out sugarpaste and shape into a pillow. Allow to dry. Paint the pillow with contrasting stripes using edible food colouring.*

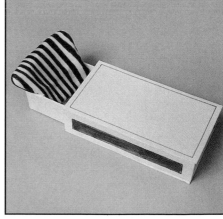

9 *Place the pillow in the open drawer of the matchbox and fix with royal icing.*

10 **HAT:** *Make a cone of red almond paste. Flatten a sugarpaste ball, making it larger than the hat base, and fold it up over the cone. Make and attach a sugarpaste pom-pom.*

11 *Fix the Mummy and Daddy mouse to pillow using royal icing. Make arms and hands from almond paste. Decorate as required.*

12 *Make a sugarpaste cover and frill the edges (see page 46). Place the baby mice under the cover on the base at the end of the matchbox. Decorate as required.*

Tucked up in their matchbox, these mice will amuse adults and children at Christmas time. The novelty would make an ideal centre table decoration and could have tiny presents placed inside the drawer.

Gardening Cake

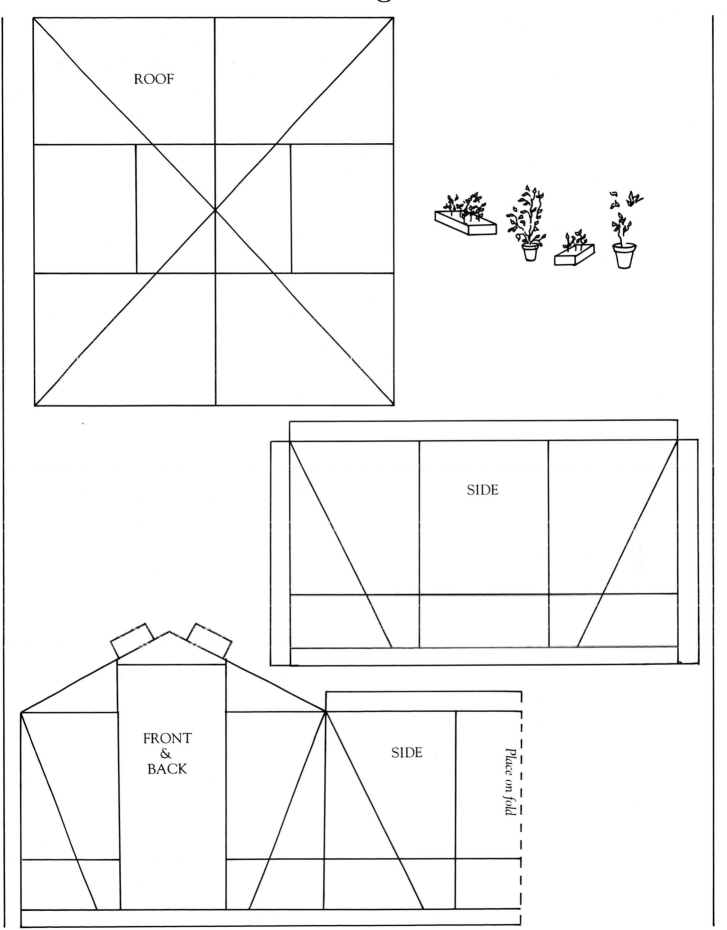

ROOF

SIDE

FRONT
&
BACK

SIDE

Place on fold

1 Using approved food pens, draw and colour a border for the cake onto the smooth side of rice paper.

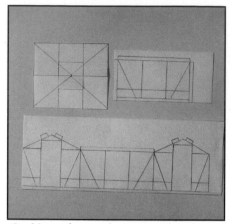

2 Using the templates as guides, draw or trace the greenhouse outline onto the smooth side of rice paper, using a brown food pen. Do not cut out until drawings are complete.

3 Draw, or trace, pots of flowers and boxes of seeds, etc. to fill the shelves along the sides of the greenhouse. Colour the drawings, as shown.

4 Cut around edges. To form first corner, place the blunt side of a knife between front and side of greenhouse and bend the paper along dotted line.

5 Fix the greenhouse side to the front by moistening the side flap with a paintbrush dampened with water.

6 Finally, cut out door, taking care not to tear bottom edge. Repairs can be made by attaching a piece of rice paper dampened with water, to inside of greenhouse.

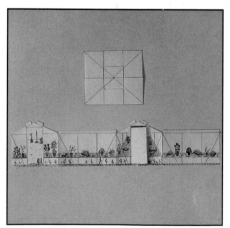

7 Bend the roof in half using the blunt side of a knife. Cut a window in the roof.

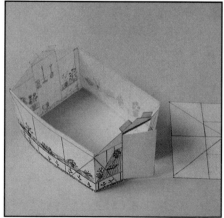

8 Using the blunt side of a knife, bend the paper at the final corner to form a rectangle. Moisten the flap with water and join the sides.

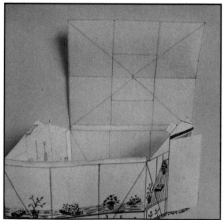

9 Moisten one top flap with water and fix one side of the roof. Repeat for the other side.

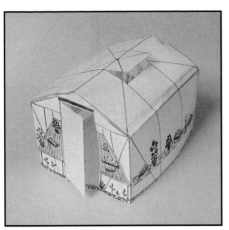

10 Stand the greenhouse in an up-right position and leave to dry for approximately 10 minutes.

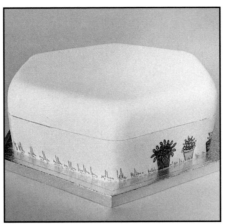

11 Fix the decorated border to the base of the cake using a little piping gel.

12 Draw, and cut, a path from rice paper. Fix to cake-top with piping gel. Cut a wheelbarrow and flowers, with tabs, from rice paper and fix in the same way.

A cake such as this would be a novel idea for a gardening enthusiast, especially if decorated with the person's favourite flowers or vegetables. The name is made from flower paste blossoms.

Decorative Frills and Flounces

Elaine Garrett of South Africa first produced the frill using template **A**. The other templates are variations on the theme.

1 **GARRETT FLOUNCE:** Roll out sugarpaste and cut a shape using template **A**. To enable the paste to slide, dust a small amount of cornflour onto the work surface.

2 Place a cocktail stick flat on the surface with the tapered end over the edge of the circle. Rock the cocktail stick back and forth to create the frill.

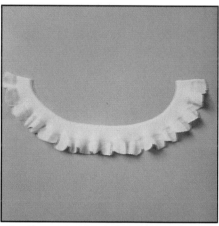

3 Cut across one side of the circle, dampen with a little water, and attach the flounce to the cake, as required.

4 **DIFFERENT FRILLS:** Roll out sugarpaste and cut 1 shape using template **B** (see page 47). Cut the shape down the centre and mark, with a knife, the depth of the frill required.

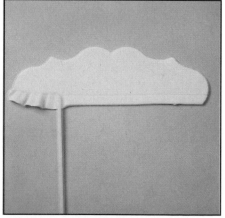

5 Dust a little cornflour on the work surface and flute the cut edge with a plain cocktail stick.

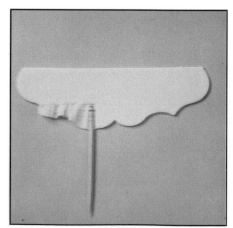

6 Alternatively, dust a little cornflour on the work surface and flute the curved edge with a grooved cocktail stick.

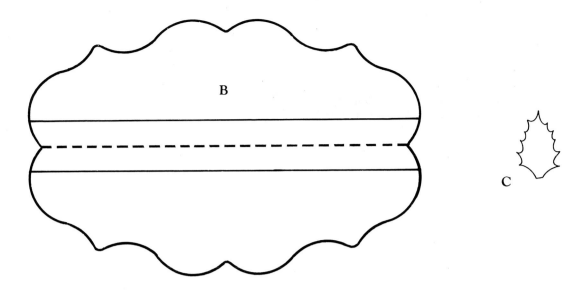

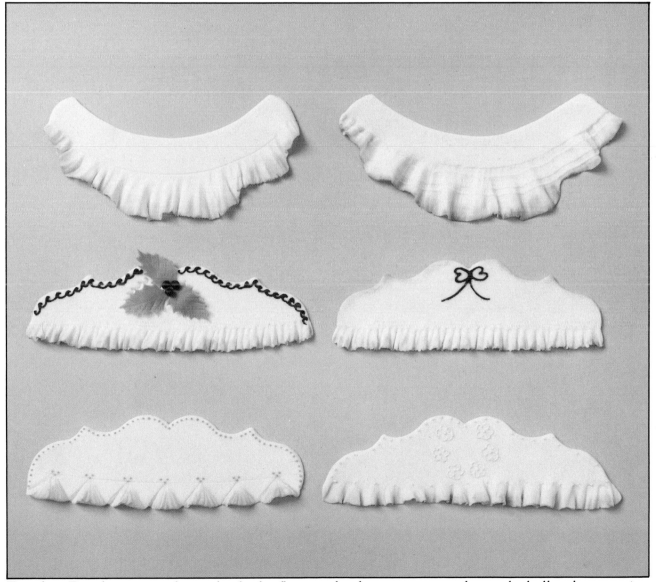

Template **B** makes a very elegant border by fluting either the cut or curved edge. For a Christmas border, cut out and attach holly shapes using template **C**.

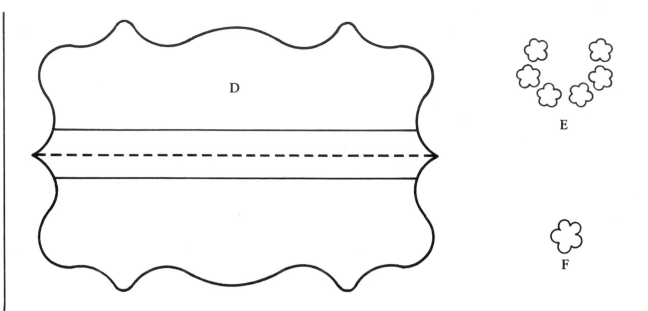

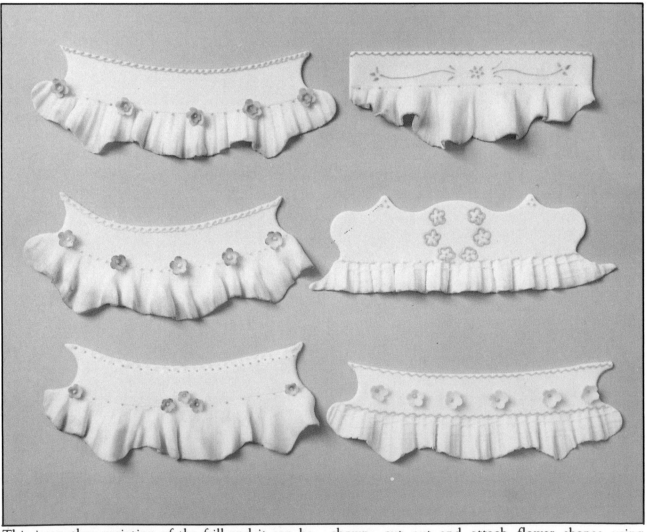

This is another variation of the frill and it can be decorated in a variety of ways. To decorate as shown, cut out and attach flower shapes using templates **E** and **F**.

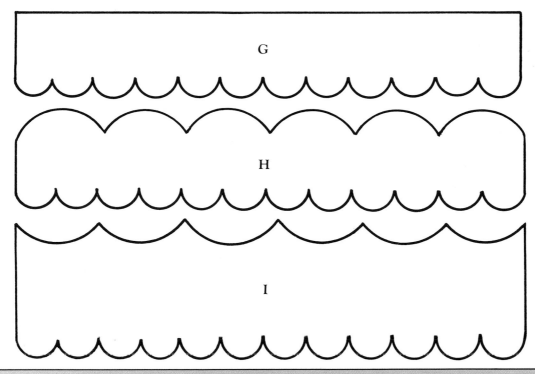

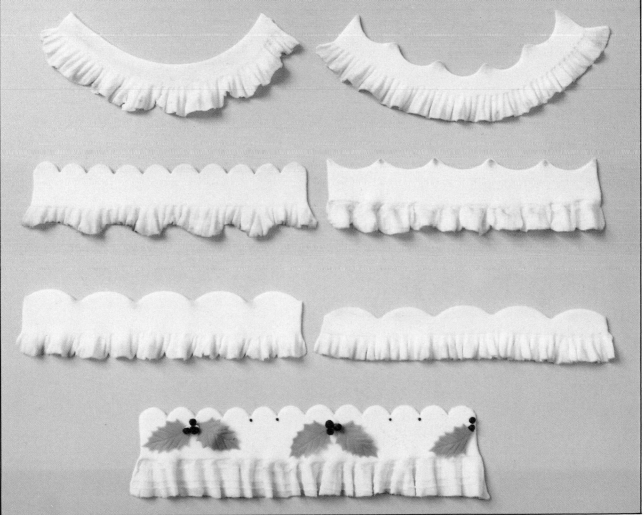

Using templates **G**, **H** and **I**, different effects can be obtained by fluting either the top or the bottom of the shapes. Templates **H** and **I** can also have a straight edge.

7 Cut sugarpaste using template **B** (see page 47). Cut in half and flute cut edge with a cocktail stick. Use template **C** (see page 47) for holly shapes and make a Christmas tree (see pages 84-85).

8 Cut sugarpaste using template **H** (see page 49) and flute lower edge. Cut out flowers using template **F** (see page 48). Fix onto border with royal icing. Decorate cake-top (see pages 61-63).

9 Cut out sugarpaste using template **G** (see page 49). Press out each scallop into a fan shape using a cocktail stick approximately 8 times. When dry, over-pipe edge with royal icing.

Using template **A** (see page 46) this Garrett Flounce border looks very attractive on any cake and can be coloured and decorated with ribbon as shown.

Mermaid Cake

SUGAR ROCKS

Ingredients

Granulated sugar 905g (2lb)
Water 250ml (8oz)
Royal icing* 100g (3½oz)

* Colour the royal icing first if coloured rocks are required.

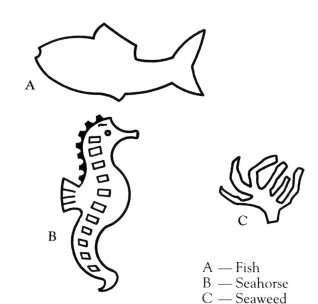

A — Fish
B — Seahorse
C — Seaweed

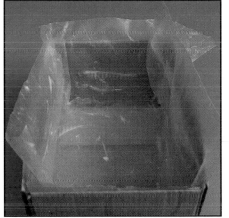

1 **SUGAR ROCKS:** *Line a cardboard box with greased waxed paper. Use a box approximately 25.5cm x 20.5cm x 10cm (10" x 8" x 4") for 905g (2lb) of sugar.*

2 *Place the water and sugar in a saucepan and boil rapidly until a temperature of 138°C (280°F) is reached. A sugar thermometer is essential for this step.*

3 *Remove the saucepan from the heat and stir in the well-beaten royal icing.*

4 *Continue stirring the royal icing until the mixture bubbles and rises.*

5 *Quickly pour the mixture into the cardboard box. (It will roughly double its volume). Leave to cool.*

6 *When the mixture is cold, cut it into pieces of appropriate sizes. The pieces can be crushed with a rolling pin to make sand.*

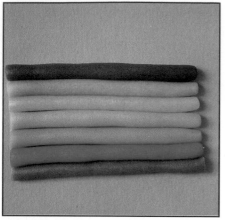

7 **FISH:** *Colour almond paste in 7 different colours. Place on a non-stick surface, without sugar, and roll each colour into a thin roll.*

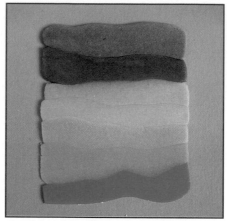

8 *Press the rolls together and roll a rolling pin over the surface so that the colours merge.*

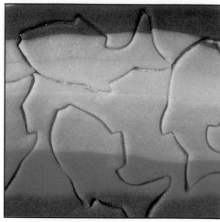

9 *Cut out fish shapes using template **A**. Place the template at various angles to give each fish a different colouring.*

10 *Mark scales with a straw, and indent fins and tail with a knife. Mark eye sockets with a ball tool and pipe the eyes with royal icing.*

11 **MERMAID:** *Colour almond paste to a flesh colour. Make balls of almond paste for the body **A**, head **B** and arms **C**, diminishing in size, as shown.*

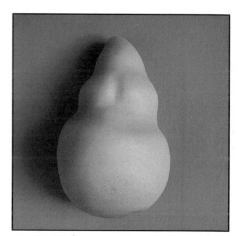

12 *Make a cone from the largest ball **A**. Indent for the top of the chest and waist with the outside of a little finger. Shape breasts with a ball tool.*

13 *Roll the lower part of the body, elongating the almond paste to a point for the tail.*

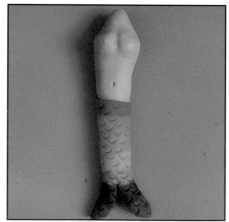

14 *Repeat steps **7-8** and wrap the almond paste around the body. Cut and part the tail. Mark scales with a drinking straw and indent the navel with a cocktail stick.*

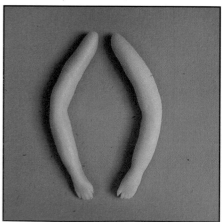

15 *Make the arms and hands from the 2 small balls of almond paste **C** (see page 14). Moisten the arms and head with a little water and fix to the body.*

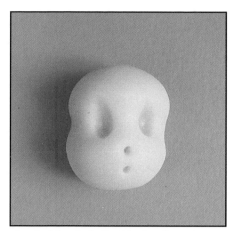

16 Use the ball of flesh coloured almond paste **B** to make the head (see pages 13-14).

17 Pipe the hair with royal icing and make 2 tiny balls of almond paste for the nipples. Dust the face and body with petal dust. Decorate hair with almond paste seaweed, using template **C**.

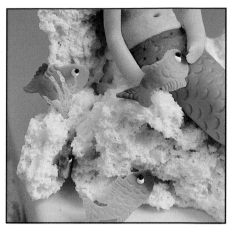

18 Using template **B**, trace and draw seahorse onto rice paper. Colour the design and cut out. Arrange and fix all pieces with royal icing.

A colourful mermaid cake such as this would appeal to any age group. For the fisherman it would be the one that got away! The sugar rocks and coloured fish complete the scene.

Making Moulds

The following items are required for making moulds (or leaf veiners):

Milliput epoxy resin putty, standard grade
Petroleum jelly
Masking tape 5cm (2") wide
Shallow tray
Well veined, fresh leaves, cleaned and dried.

Mouldings can be made from any size of fresh leaf as they come into season. The advantage of making moulds is that once made they can be used throughout the year whether fresh leaves are available or not.

For future reference, always write the name of the leaf on the mould using a washable pen.

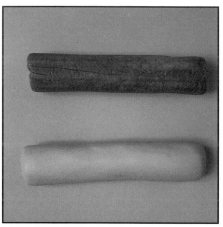

1 MAKING THE MOULDS: *Cut equal amounts of Milliput putty from each pack, according to size of leaf. Rub a little petroleum jelly into hands and knead the 2 pieces together.*

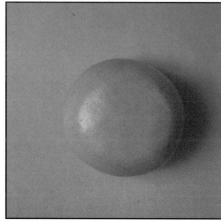

2 *When the 2 pieces are thoroughly mixed, and of an even colour, roll the putty into a ball and flatten.*

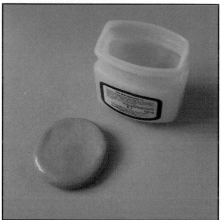

3 *Apply a very thin layer of petroleum jelly to top. Place a length of masking tape, longer than the leaf, in the tray, sticky side up. Secure ends with small pieces of tape.*

4 PRIMROSE LEAF: *Leaving a stalk for easy handling, place the face of the leaf onto the sticky tape. Smooth out from the centre to remove air bubbles and creases.*

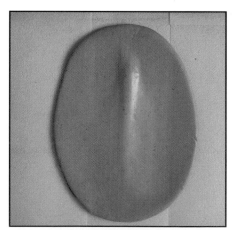

5 *Take the side of the putty with the petroleum jelly and place it over the leaf, pressing well in. Apply petroleum jelly to the top and leave to set.*

6 *For economy, the upper surface can be used to make another mould by placing a second leaf, vein side down, onto the putty. Smooth out from the centre.*

7 Remove the leaf from the top of the mould, and allow the putty to harden overnight. This will be used as the female mould.

8 To make a male mould, repeat steps *1-2*. Apply petroleum jelly to the top and press this surface into the female mould. Leave to dry.

9 When the putty is dry, release the male mould. The 2 halves are now ready to create realistic leaves.

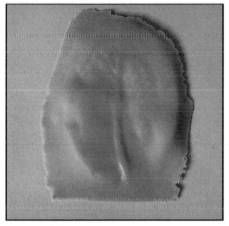

10 MAKING FLOWER PASTE LEAVES: Roll out green flower paste and press it well down onto the top of the mould.

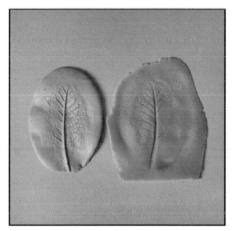

11 Peel off the flower paste to reveal a perfectly moulded leaf.

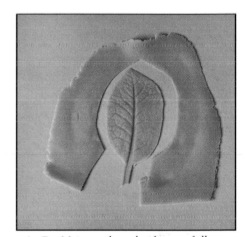

12 Using a sharp knife, carefully cut around the leaf shape.

13 Place the leaf on a cornflour-dusted sponge and soften the edges with a ball-shaped modelling tool.

14 Transfer the leaf to a piece of shaped foam to bend and curl it into shape.

15 Picture shows the realistic flower paste leaves adding the finishing touch to a posy of primroses.

Fairy Cake

Filigree Butterfly Wings

1 **BUTTERFLY: Wings** *Trace the wings and attach the design to a tile, or perspex, with masking tape. Tape a sheet of easy-off plastic on top.*

2 *Pipe the inside design with royal icing, starting at the top (No. 00). Continue by piping the outside and leave to dry for 24 hours.*

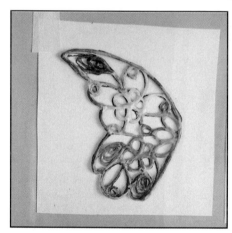

3 *Paint various colours onto the wings with food colours, using a No. 0 paintbrush.*

4 **Body** *Pipe a bulb of royal icing (No. 2), releasing pressure for neck. Continue with another bulb, pulling icing down and gradually releasing pressure. Fix 2 stamens in head for antennae.*

5 *While the icing is still soft, fix the wings into the body. Support with a small piece of foam and leave to dry.*

6 *When the butterfly is dry, paint the body and leave to dry for 2 hours. Remove the foam and fix to the cake with royal icing.*

Flowers

A — Primrose
B — Primrose Calyx
C — Violet
D — Violet Calyx
E — Skirt
F — Wings
G — Hat

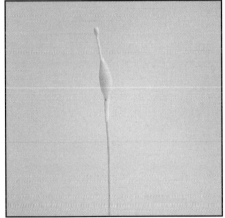

7 PRIMROSE: *Tape 1 yellow stamen to end of a 26 gauge wire. Using rose water or gum arabic, fix a small piece of flower paste to bottom of stamen. Leave to dry.*

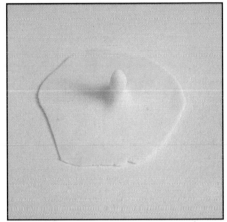

8 *Make a 'golf-tee' of flower paste and finger out around the base. Thin out the flat end by rolling with a cable knitting needle.*

9 *Using template A, or a cutter, cut out a flower, complete with throat.*

10 *Soften the edges with a ball tool. Push a cocktail stick well down the throat and roll between fingers to thin down the flower paste.*

11 *Apply rose water or gum arabic glue to the paste on the wire and push wire into throat until the end of the stamen is just below opening in centre.*

12 *Roll out green flower paste and cut out a calyx using template B, or a cutter. Cut off 2 sepals. Cut down the centre of 2 adjacent sepals and spread out.*

13 To cup, ball towards centre with a balling tool, and vein with a veining tool (see page 64). Apply a little rose water to base of stem and wrap calyx round.

14 *Bud* Make a yellow flower paste cone. Push moistened end of a 30 gauge white wire through centre. Wrap moistened green flower paste around bud. Pinch 5 grooves to represent calyx.

15 Petal dust primrose bud stalks pink, and flower stalks green. Make primrose leaves (see pages 54-55). Tape leaves and flowers together in pretty arrangement.

16 VIOLET: Make a 'golf-tee' of white flower paste and flatten base. Using template **C** (see page 57), or a cutter, cut out flower. Soften edges with a ball tool.

17 Moisten the end of a hooked 30 gauge wire with rose water or gum arabic glue. Fix the wire into the top of the flower, behind the petals. Leave to dry.

18 Roll out green flower paste and cut out using template **D** (see page 57), or a cutter. Soften the edges with a ball tool and stroke sepals from tip to centre.

19 Moisten calyx with rose water or gum arabic glue. Thread wire onto calyx centre and onto back of petals. Paint 'face' with a No.000 paintbrush and petal dust flower.

20 *Bud* Make a cone of flower paste. Repeat step **17**. Paint calyx with edible food colouring using a No.000 paintbrush and leave to dry.

21 Make violet leaves using a mould (see page 54). Tape flowers and leaves together to make a decorative arrangement.

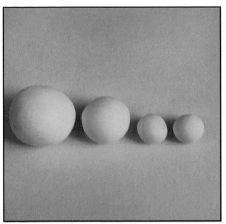

22 **Fairy:** *Make 4 balls of Mexican paste for the body* **A**, *head* **B** *and arms* **C**, *diminishing in size, as shown.*

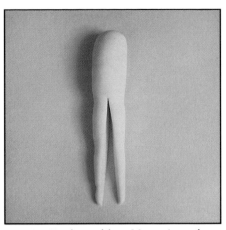

23 **Body and legs** *Using* **A**, *make an elongated cone. Make 3 indentations for top of legs, knee and ankle. Cut lengthways to top of leg.*

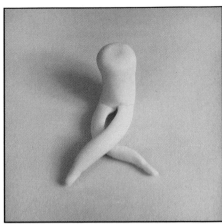

24 *Bend legs to required position. Support the body against a piece of foam and leave to dry.*

25 **Skirt** *Roll out coloured flower paste and cut out 1 shape using template* **E** *(see page 57), or a cutter. Frill the edges (see page 46). Cut out a circle from centre.*

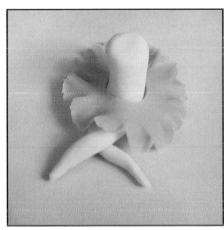

26 *Moisten the underside of the skirt with a little rose water and fix into position.*

27 **Bodice** *Roll out a rectangle of coloured flower paste and cut 1 bodice.*

28 *Moisten the lower sides of the body and fold over the bodice, pressing in at the side and leaving 2 openings for the arms.*

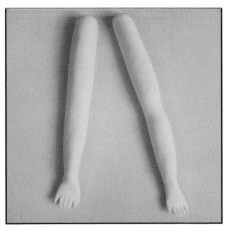

29 **Arms** *Make 2 thin arms from the Mexican paste balls* **C** *(see page 14).*

30 **Head** *Using* **B** *make a head and face (see pages 13-14). Fix with royal icing. Pipe hair with royal icing (No. 2).*

31 Merge rolls of coloured flower paste (see page 52). **Wings** Cut using template **F** (see page 57). **Hat** Cut and frill flower paste using template **G** (see page 57). Place small ball in centre.

32 Fix the wings on the back of the fairy using royal icing.

33 Petal dust the edges of the skirt and hat. Fix to the board with royal icing.

This enchanting sugarcraft piece is a child's dream cake, the delicate filigree butterfly being fed by Primrose Lil.

The lifelike flowers add a realistic touch to the woodland scene.

Heart-shaped Cake

Cover a cake board (see page 12). Decorate the cake-side with frills and fix sprays of flowers to the top. Fix a single rose on the base of the cake board.

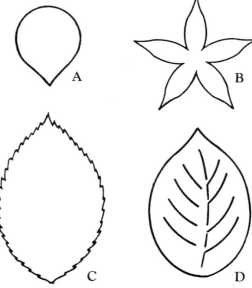

A — Rose Petal
B — Rose Calyx
C — Rose Leaf
D — Rose Veins

1 OPEN BUD: *Using a little rose water, fit a small cone of coloured flower paste onto the hooked end of a 26 gauge wire. The cone should be smaller than the petal length.*

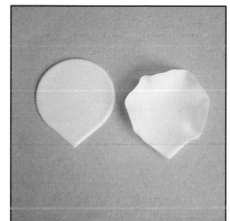

2 *Roll out paste and cut 2 petals using template A, or a cutter. Thin the edges before placing on a sponge and cupping the petals with a ball-shaped modelling tool.*

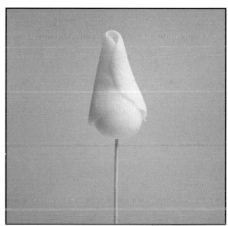

3 *Moisten the cone. Take the first petal and wrap it around the cone, covering it completely, but keeping the top slightly open.*

4 *Moisten cone with rose water and fold second petal opposite the first with its centre over the join of the first petal. Cut out 3 more petals and repeat step 2.*

5 *Moisten the side edge of the third petal. Positioning its centre over the join of the second petal, wrap it round, a little higher than the first 2 petals.*

6 *Using a little rose water, moisten the open side of the third petal, and on one side of the fourth petal. Repeat for fifth petal so that the last 3 petals interlock.*

7 *Cut out the calyx from green flower paste, using template **B**, or a cutter. Place the calyx on a sponge and cup its centre with a ball-shaped modelling tool.*

8 *Moisten the base of the bud. Thread the wire through the centre of the calyx, gently pressing the calyx onto the petals to complete the bud.*

9 **FLOWER:** *Make a bud as in steps **1-6**. Add an extra 4 or 5 petals in the same way, but positioning slightly lower. Bend over the top edges slightly.*

10 *Repeat steps **7-8** to complete the rose.*

11 *Roll out flower paste leaving a thick part at base. Cut 1 leaf. Moisten end of 28 gauge wire with rose water and insert tip into leaf. Vein and soften edges with a ball tool.*

12 *Make 2 more leaves in the same way and tape them together with the rose. Dust the leaves and petals to colour of choice.*

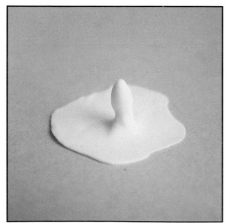

13 **FANTASY FLOWER:** *Make a 'golf-tee' of flower paste. Thin out the wide end by rolling with a cable needle, leaving a centre stem, as shown.*

14 *Cut the petals, using template **B** as a guide, or by placing a cutter over the stem.*

15 *Place the flower onto a sponge, or in cornflour-dusted hands, and shape the back of the petals inwards using a ball-shaped modelling tool.*

16 Tape 1 long stamen and 3 short stamens to 28 gauge wire, as shown.

17 Moisten the tape and thread the wire through the centre of the flower until the moistened tape is embedded in the flower.

18 Hold the flower at the base where it meets the stem and bend the wire at this point. Dust with colour of choice.

An impressive cake such as this, with its dramatic but subtle colouring, is suitable for any loved one, be it for an engagement, a valentine or an anniversary. The Garrett Flounce (see page 46) adds the finishing touch.

Making a Petal Veiner

Using an epoxy resin putty, such as Milliput, mix 2 small pieces of the putty together and wrap a piece round the handle end of a paintbrush. Mould it into a cone shape and, while it is still soft, mark with a corn husk and leave to set.

A — Freesia and Daffodil Petal
B — Freesia Calyx
C — Daffodil Sepal

1 **FREESIA:** *Cut off the head of a stamen, soften it in water, flatten, and fan it out. Cut end into 4 or 5 sections and tape onto 26 gauge wire with shorter stamens.*

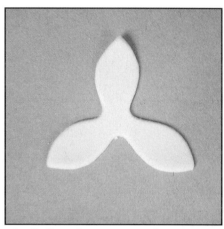

2 *Roll out flower paste and cut out one flat set of petals using template* **A** *or cutter. Soften the edges with a ball tool.*

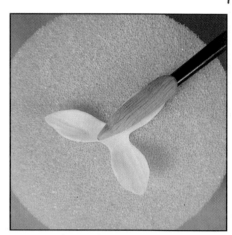

3 *Lay the petal on a cornflour-dusted sponge. Vein by laying the veining tool along the length of each petal, rolling lightly from side to side to round the petals.*

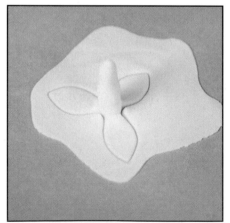

4 *Make a 'golf-tee' of flower paste and gently flatten the base, leaving a thin throat. Cut a second set of petals using template* **A** *or cutter.*

5 *Shape the petals with a ball-shaped modelling tool.*

6 *Push the veiner down the throat and press against a thumb to thin out the paste.*

7 Moisten the centre of the first set of petals with rose water. Fix the second set of petals in between the first and hollow out the centre with the veiner.

8 Moisten the tape at the base of the stamen with rose water. Push the wire down into the throat and roll between the fingers to thin the paste. Hang upside down to dry.

9 Roll out green flower paste and cut a calyx using template **B**. Cut off 3 sepals. Cut off tips and soften edges. Moisten with rose water and wrap around flower base.

10 **DAFFODIL:** Select 1 long and 6 short stamens. Tape onto a length of 26 gauge wire with the shorter stamens lying just below the base of the longer stamen.

11 **Trumpet** Make a roll of dark yellow flower paste. The trumpet can be in different sizes according to the type of daffodil.

12 Push a cocktail stick into the trumpet centre and thin out the edges by pressing firmly against a fore-finger. Place on a board and flute the outer edge (see page 46).

13 Moisten the base of the stamens with a little rose water and push the wire through the trumpet centre. Squeeze the base of the trumpet and leave to dry.

14 **Flower** Repeat steps **2-3** for the first set of petals. Make a second set in pale yellow paste by repeating steps **4-6**.

15 Moisten the centre of the first set of petals with rose water. Fix the second set of petals in between the first and hollow out the centre with the veiner.

16 Moisten the inside with a little rose water and thread the dry trumpet through the centre. Thin the paste by rolling between the fingers. Remove excess.

17 When dry, dust the base with pale green petal dust. Thread a small ball of green flower paste onto the base of the flower and join by rolling between the fingers.

18 *Sepal* Roll out light brown flower paste. Cut a sepal using template C and vein (see step **3**). Moisten base of flower with rose water and wrap sepal around.

Different flowers can be used to complement the seasons to make this an eye-catching cake for Easter, birthdays or anniversaries. A joy to behold. Be careful, this might go to your head!

Pandora Cake

Low Relief

This is a quick and easy technique for decorating the top or side of a cake.

The technique usually consists of pressing paste into a cornflour-dusted mould. The moulded piece is then decorated and coloured before being applied to the cake.

Various mediums can be used, such as sugarpaste, flower paste, Mexican paste, almond paste and chocolate paste. The first four can be decorated with royal icing.

A — Carnation Petal
B — Large Calyx
C — Small Calyx

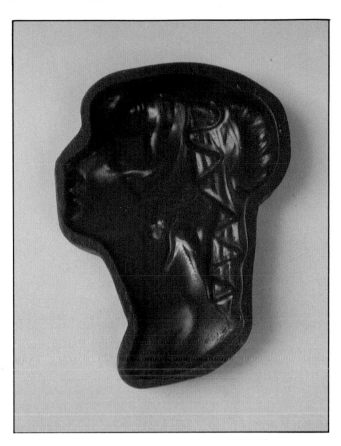

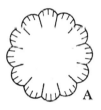 A   B C

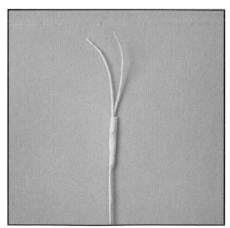

1 **CARNATION:** *Fold a stamen in half and cut off the ends. Tape the ends to a length of 26/28 gauge wire.*

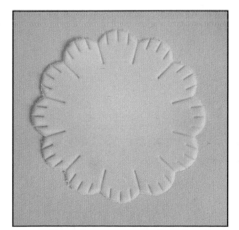

2 *Roll out flower paste and cut 2 or 3 petal shapes using template A or cutter. The number of shapes depends on the fullness of the carnation.*

3 *Frill the edges of the petal with a cocktail stick (see page 46).*

4 Moisten the tape with a little rose water and thread the wire through the centre of the petal.

5 Fold the petal in half, ensuring that any pressure is on the join only.

6 Moisten the centre with rose water and fold one-third of the petal to the front of the flower.

7 Moisten the centre back with rose water and fold the other third to the back, squeezing the paste at the base of the flower.

8 Apply rose water to base, and slightly higher in places. Insert wire through the centre of second petal, moisten and squeeze round centre of first petal.

9 *Calyx* Cut a calyx using template **B**. Cut off the tips and soften edges. Moisten the carnation base with rose water and thread wire through the centre of calyx.

10 Roll out pale green flower paste and cut a calyx using template **C**. Cut off the tips and soften edges. Thread the wire through the centre and fix to calyx **B**.

11 **FIGURE HEAD:** Press flesh coloured sugarpaste into a cornflour-dusted mould. Carefully remove the paste from the mould and leave to dry.

12 Paint the features with edible colouring. Dust the cheeks and neck with petal dust and pipe the hair with royal icing. Fix tiny flower paste flowers to hair.

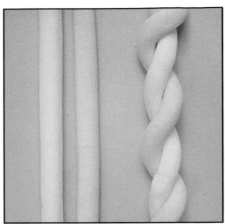

13 *Collar* Roll out sugarpaste and cut a strip for the collar. Frill the edges with a cocktail stick (see page 46). Fix to neck with royal icing and dust when dry.

14 WINDOW: Moisten strips of rice paper with water to form window panes. Arrange on cake when dry. Cut a sugarpaste moon and fix to cake-top with carnation and girl, using royal icing.

15 ROPE: Make 2 rolls of different coloured sugarpaste. Twist the rolls together to form a rope, and fix to the base of the cake.

The Pandora cake incorporates rice paper, sugarpaste and flower paste, and is very simple and quick to make. It would be an ideal cake for a teenage girl, or to celebrate a coming-of-age or an engagement.

A

C

D

B

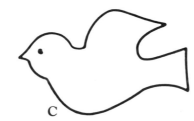

C

D

A — Small Blossom
B — Large Blossom
C — Bird
D — Wing

1 **LACE EDGING:** *Make templates* **A** *and* **B** *or use cutters. Roll out sugarpaste and cut out blossom flowers of each size, 2 at a time.*

2 *Cut off 3 petals from each blossom. The smaller halves will decorate the top edge of the cake and the larger ones will decorate the base.*

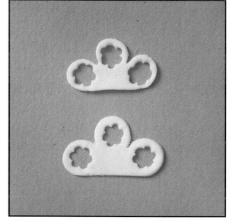

3 *Cut out the centre of each petal, using a small blossom cutter, or a piping tube. Fix the lace pieces to the cake with royal icing.*

4 **BIRDS:** *Roll out sugarpaste. Using templates* **C** *and* **D**, *make 4 birds with separate wings, 2 in reverse. Cut out and complete the birds one at a time.*

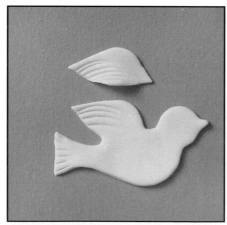

5 *Indent the wings with the edge of a round cutter and shape the separate wing. Mark the tail feathers with the back of a knife. Leave to dry for 1 hour.*

6 *Dust the bird with petal dust to add colour. Paint the eye with food colouring using a No. 000 paintbrush. Fix the separate wing to the bird with royal icing.*

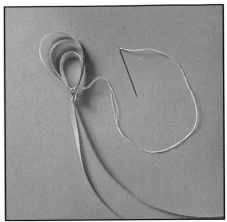

7 **BLOSSOMS:** *Roll out flower paste and cut a number of small blossoms.* Place on a sponge and indent each centre with a ball-shaped modelling tool.

8 *Make a ball of sugarpaste. While it is still soft, press the blossoms into the ball and fix with a little royal icing.*

9 *Form loops of ribbon of varying heights and secure with a few stitches.* Using tweezers, push the ribbon into the floral ball and fix with royal icing.

Elegant, but simple, this cake has a sugarpaste lace edge which is easy to make. The decoration could be used for any anniversary and would make an ideal single-tier wedding cake.

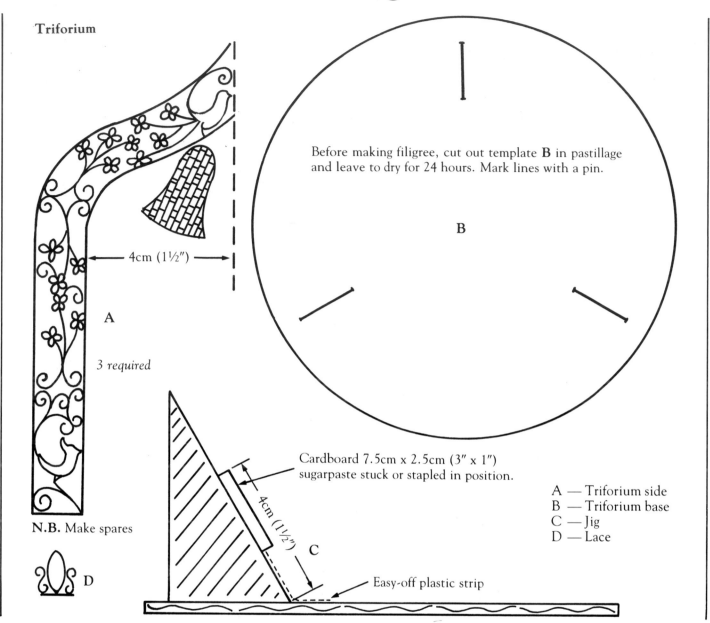

Triforium

4cm (1½")

A

3 required

N.B. Make spares

D

Before making filigree, cut out template **B** in pastillage and leave to dry for 24 hours. Mark lines with a pin.

B

Cardboard 7.5cm x 2.5cm (3" x 1") sugarpaste stuck or stapled in position.

4cm (1½")

C

Easy-off plastic strip

A — Triforium side
B — Triforium base
C — Jig
D — Lace

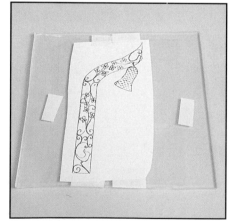

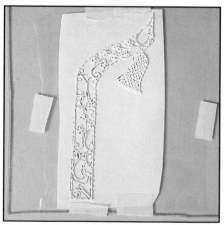

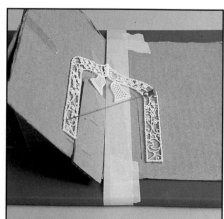

1 **(a)** *Fix design with masking tape to sheet of perspex, or tile. Tape easy-off plastic sheet on top.* **(b)** *For easy assembly, use template* **C** *to make a cardboard 'jig' (see step* **3***).*

2 *Pipe inside of design with royal icing (No.0). Pipe outline using tear-drops of royal icing. Leave to dry. Turn over and pipe outline again for strength. Make at least 4.*

3 *Fix easy-off plastic down fold of 'jig'. Slide a thin palette knife under 2 dry pieces* **A** *and place into position on jig. Pipe royal icing down top edges to join. Leave to dry.*

4 Fix paintbrush in support position. Pipe royal icing on 2 marks on dry base **B** and on base of 2 pieces **A**. Tip jig up and lift into position with pins. Leave to dry.

5 Pipe royal icing onto remaining mark on base **B**, and base and top of third piece **A**. Place hat pin through strongest piece of filigree and lift into position.

6 Using template **D**, repeat step **1a**. Pipe lace centre first, then scrolls and base line. When dry, remove with palette knife and fix around base **B** with royal icing.

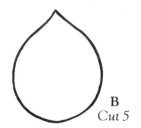

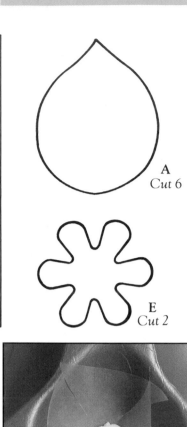

A
Cut 6

B
Cut 5

C
Cut 4

D
Cut 4

A-E — Petals

F — Calyx

E
Cut 2

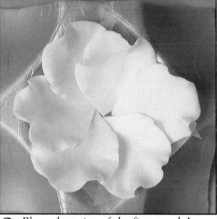

F
Cut 1

7 **PREPARATION:** *Roll out flower paste thinly and cut out petals using templates* **A-D**, *or cutters. Soften edges with a ball tool and cup on a dusted sponge. Leave to dry for 24 hours.*

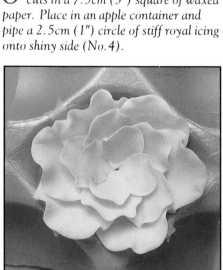

8 **OPEN FLOWER:** *Make 4 diagonal cuts in a 7.5cm (3") square of waxed paper. Place in an apple container and pipe a 2.5cm (1") circle of stiff royal icing onto shiny side (No.4).*

9 *Place the point of the first petal* **A** *onto the circle. Repeat with the remaining* **A** *petals, overlapping each petal and tucking the last one under the first.*

10 *Pipe another circle of royal icing on top of the* **A** *petals. Repeat step* **8** *with the* **B** *petals, starting with the centre of a petal over a join.*

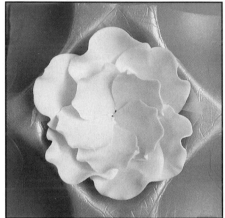

11 *Repeat step* **10** *with the* **C** *petals.*

12 *Repeat step* **10** *with the* **D** *petals. Pipe a little royal icing in the centre and cut 5 or 7 stamens. Place in the centre using tweezers.*

13 *When the flower is completely dry, petal dust the edges. Remove the wax paper. Holding the flowers by the stamens, transfer to the cake and fix with royal icing.*

14 FUCHSIA: *Wire 1 long stamen and 6 short stamens onto a 26 gauge wire. Make as many as required.*

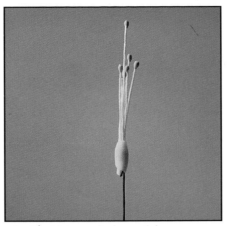

15 *Moisten the base of the stamens with rose water or gum arabic glue, and roll a small piece of flower paste onto the base. Leave to dry for 30 minutes.*

16 *Roll out flower paste and cut the flower shape using template* **E**, *or a cutter. Frill alternate petals.*

17 *Turn the paste over and frill the remainder of the petals.*

18 *Moisten the paste at base of the stamens and thread the wire through the centre of the petals. Press gently at the base and leave upside down to dry.*

19 *Repeat steps* **15-16**. *Moisten first set of petals a quarter of the way up. Place in centre of second set, using petal edge as a guide. Press base gently. Leave upside down to dry.*

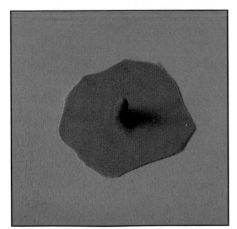

20 *Make a 'golf tee' from flower paste and flatten the base. Using template* **F**, *or a cutter, cut one shape. Soften and ball (see page 64).*

21 *Moisten the centre of the calyx a quarter of the way up each sepal. Thread the flower into the centre and arrange around the flower. Roll between fingers to thin.*

22 *Roll a ball of flower paste. Moisten the base and thread wire through the centre of the ball. Roll between fingers to merge into base.*

23 **Bottom Tier:** *Place a piece of sugarpaste on top of the cake and fix the fuchsia stems into the paste. Fix 3 open roses onto the cake with royal icing.*

24 **Middle tier:** *Repeat step 22. Fix 2 open roses onto the cake with royal icing.*

25 *Fix rose in triforium with royal icing. Fix fuchsia stem in ball of sugarpaste. Place triforium on top and level with small pieces of sugarpaste opposite fuchsia.*

This unusual wedding cake, with flowers arranged in a Hogarth Curve, and the delicate triforium, would appeal to many brides. The assembly 'jig' for the triforium (see page 72) plays an essential part in the construction.

Angelina the Bride

Free-standing Moulded Figures

This is an ever-popular and versatile technique which can be used for humorous as well as formal figures.

There are various types of moulds on the market, including plastic and perspex.

One of the difficulties is to avoid making the figure look too rigid. This can be overcome when removing the soft figure from the mould by bending it to the required shape. The idea is to introduce apparent movement into the figure.

Leave it to dry on cornflour-dusted foam, or propped into position. For an upright position, leave the figure lying prone.

Avoid leaving non-edible supports in the figure, such as cocktail sticks, wire or skewers.

*P*icture shows both halves of a plastic mould in the shape of a woman's torso.

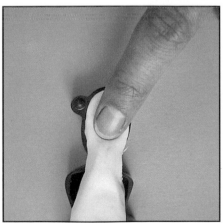

1 **TORSO:** *Push flesh coloured Mexican paste into the cornflour-dusted mould, pressing it firmly into the face portion to fill in the features.*

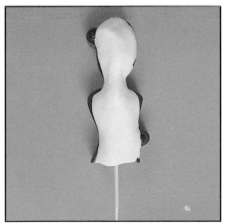

2 *For easy handling, insert a cocktail stick into the paste, pushing it right through the body and into the head section.*

3 *Place the back of the mould onto the top of the paste and press firmly together. Trim off surplus paste.*

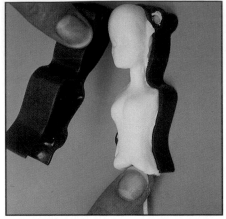

4 *Holding the stick, carefully remove the front of the mould. Cushion face in the hand and remove back in the same way. Leave to dry on a piece of cornflour-dusted foam.*

5 *When dry, paint the features with food colourings, using a No.000 paintbrush. Dust the cheeks with petal dust and remove the cocktail stick.*

6 **BODY:** *Roll out pastillage and make a cone for the body. Insert the torso into the body and leave to dry for 24 hours.*

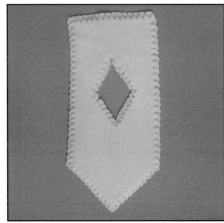

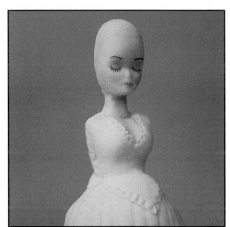

7 **SKIRT:** *Roll and cut a strip of sugarpaste. Flute with a cocktail stick (see page 46) and wrap it around body. Press in the top of folds using a blunt-ended cocktail stick.*

8 **BODICE:** *Roll out sugarpaste and cut out a shape for the bodice, as shown. Mark the edges to make a decorative border.*

9 *Place the bodice into position on the torso and fix with a little rose water.*

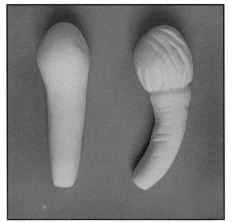

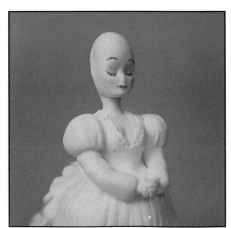

10 **TRAIN:** *Fix a roll of sugarpaste at back to provide a base. Cut a Garrett Frill and frill the edges (see page 46). Starting at base, build up layers, and tuck in sides.*

11 **SLEEVES:** *Take a ball of sugarpaste and make two-thirds into a roll. Indent for puff sleeves and folds, using the back of a knife. Make a hole in the end for hands.*

12 *Make a pair of hands (see page 14). Insert the hands into the sleeve ends and fix with royal icing. Fix the arms with royal icing and leave to dry.*

13 **BOUQUET:** *Cut a leaf from flower paste. Moisten and insert wire into one end. Leave to dry. Make blossoms and fix, with 3 tiny ribbons, to leaf with royal icing.*

14 **HAIR:** *Make long rolls of almond paste and attach to the head. Alternatively, pipe the hair in royal icing.*

15 **VEIL:** *Gather a piece of tulle fabric at the top and fix to the head with royal icing. Fix blossoms to the top of the veil. Pipe dots of royal icing on veil.*

Such a graceful and serene bride would be a talking point for a wedding party. It would enhance any wedding table, looking attractive on the top tier of the wedding cake, or left free-standing by the side.

Tulle Church

Piping on tulle produces a delicate, lacy effect, with the tulle becoming almost transparent against the piped outline because it is so fine. The tulle helps to keep the icing intact when piping shapes that would otherwise collapse.

The most suitable tulle for this type of work is brides' fine veiling as the net is very fine preventing the bulbs of icing from seeping through the holes.

For easier working, place dark coloured paper behind the tulle where possible.

Freshly made royal icing should be used for all the piped pieces.

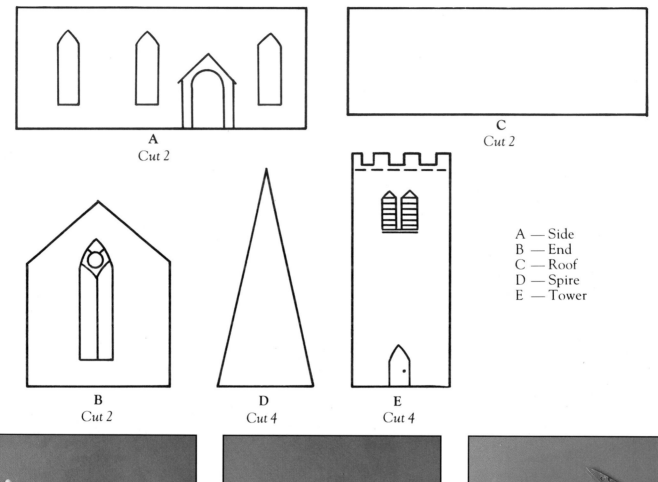

A
Cut 2

C
Cut 2

B
Cut 2

D
Cut 4

E
Cut 4

A — Side
B — End
C — Roof
D — Spire
E — Tower

1 Place a sheet of dark paper on a cake board. Pin the tulle to each template and cut around the edges.

2 Arrange the templates on the dark paper. Stick a sheet of easy-off plastic over the surface. Pin the tulle pieces taut over templates using glass-headed pins.

3 Pipe the detail in royal icing (No. 0 or 1). Pipe tiny tear-drops around outlines. When dry, remove the pieces by sliding an artist's palette knife underneath each one.

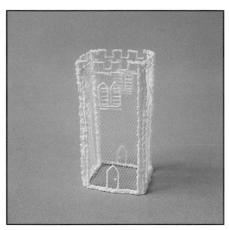

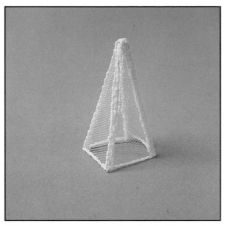

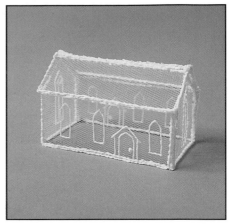

4 When assembling the pieces, insert a large hat pin through the tulle and hold the pin either side of the fabric for easy handling. Pipe joins (No. 1) with royal icing.

5 Lay a section on the plastic sheet with another alongside and support with a pin. Join with royal icing. Assemble 3 pieces. Stand up and fix the fourth side.

6 While the steeple is drying, assemble the church tower. Allow the tower to dry before fixing the steeple inside the top of the tower.

The tulle church would be an ideal way to decorate a single-tier wedding cake. It would also be suitable for a christening or confirmation. A spray of roses and satin ribbon will add the final touches.

Cover a round cake with sugarpaste and crimp the top edge while the paste is still soft. Leave to dry. Roll out a strip of sugarpaste and frill the edge with a cocktail stick (see page 46). Dampen the top edge and place around the cake-base.

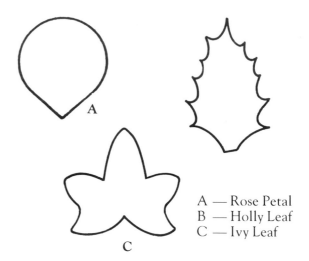

A — Rose Petal
B — Holly Leaf
C — Ivy Leaf

1 Cut 5 rose petals from flower paste using template **A**. Thin the edges with a ball tool and press out at the top of each petal to form pointed shape. Cup the centres.

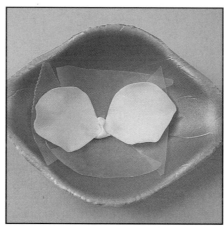

2 Cut a 6.5cm (2½") square of waxed paper cutting each corner diagonally. Pipe a bulb of royal icing in the centre of the paper and fix 2 petals, as shown.

3 Fix the third petal to the royal icing on the waxed paper, overlapping the first 2 petals.

4 Place petal 4 overlapping petal 2.

5 Place petal 5 on top of petals 1 and 4. The flower is not symmetrical.

6 Pipe a bulb of green royal icing in the centre of the flower and insert yellow-headed stamens.

*7 Roll out green flower paste and cut holly leaves using template **B**. Mark the veins. Place on a sponge and press with a ball-shaped modelling tool to curl, as shown.*

*8 Roll out red flower paste and cut the ivy leaves using template **C**. Mark the veins and soften the edges with a ball-shaped modelling tool.*

9 Fix the Christmas roses, holly and ivy leaves to the cake top, using a little royal icing.

This simple, but elegant, cake would grace any Christmas table. Decorate the base with a Garrett Frill (see pages 46-50) to give an unusual and attractive finish. The holly and ivy accentuate the festive occasion.

Christmas Tree

A — Large Calyx
B — Medium Calyx
C — Minor Calyx
D — Small Calyx
E — Star

Cut out and work on one shape at a time. 3 calyxes of each size are needed, together with 1 star shape.

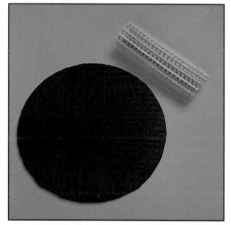

1 Fix rolled sugarpaste to a 10cm (4") diameter board using a little water. Roll a hair curler across the surface, up and down, and left to right. Trim edges.

2 TUB: Flatten the top of a sugarpaste or almond paste ball. Mark rings around sides with a knife. Push a 6.5cm (2½") length of thin spaghetti into centre and remove.

3 TREE: Roll out green flower paste and cut 3 large calyxes using template A. Place 1 shape on a cornflour-dusted sponge and cup each sepal, working from tip to centre.

4 Cut the sepals with scissors, starting at the tips, to the V. Make a small hole in the centre of each calyx.

5 Push the spaghetti into a piece of polystyrene. Thread a small ball of flower paste and 1 calyx onto the spaghetti, fixing with a little egg white or rose water.

6 Slide another small ball of paste down the spaghetti and repeat the process for the next 2 large calyxes. Ensure that the points interleave with the ones underneath.

7 *Build up the tree as in steps 3-6, using templates **B-D**, as shown. Remove the tree from the polystyrene and insert into the tub.*

8 *Roll out thick yellow flower paste and cut out a star, using template **E**, or a cutter. Holding the star between finger and thumb, ease it onto the spaghetti.*

9 *Decorate the tree with loops and bulbs of white royal icing (No. 00). When dry, paint carefully with food colours. Happy Christmas!*

A Christmas tree made from flower paste may be used on top of a cake or given as a small, edible gift. The parcels can be made from Dolly Mixtures, almond paste or sugarpaste.

Christmas Snowmen Cake

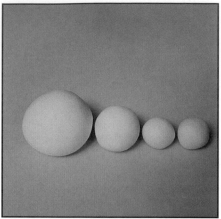

1 **SNOWMAN:** Make 4 balls of sugar-paste for body **A**, head **B** and arms **C**, diminishing in size as shown. For a firmer consistency, mix extra icing sugar into the sugarpaste.

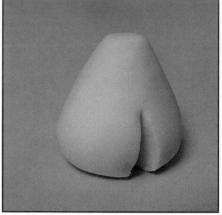

2 **Body** Roll the largest ball **A** into a cone shape and flatten the top to form a base for the head. To form the legs, make a cut in the body, as shown.

3 **Face** Make features from coloured sugarpaste. Indent head **B** for nose and mouth. Fix features using a damp paintbrush. Make hole in centre of mouth with a cocktail stick.

4 Stand snowman's body on a sugar-free, non-stick board. Fix on the head. Make buttons from 2 flattened balls of sugarpaste. Fix to body using a damp paintbrush.

5 **Scarf** Roll and cut strips of coloured almond paste. Place side by side and join by rolling again. Cut and join into a long line. Cut fringes with scissors.

6 **Hat** Make the brim by placing a ball of almond paste in a plastic bag. Flatten until the edges are very thin. Leave a thicker centre for easy removal from bag.

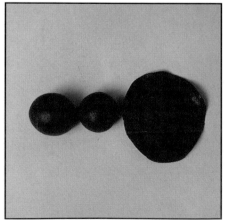

7 Make a smaller ball of almond paste for the centre of the hat. Flatten the ball slightly and fix to the brim.

8 Place the hat on top of the head. Wrap the scarf around the snowman's neck, fixing it into place with a little water.

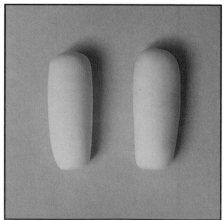

9 **Arms** Form a thick roll for each arm from the remaining 2 balls of sugar-paste **C**.

10 Fix the arms to the sides of the body using a little water. Cut out a carol book from rice paper and place in the snowman's hands.

11 Make 2 smaller snowmen following steps *1-10*. Moisten the large snowman's arms and fix them to the shoulders of the 2 smaller snowmen.

12 Place a stencil on top of the cake. Using a knife, spread firm royal icing over the stencil. Remove the stencil carefully. When dry, paint the lettering with colour.

Three jolly singing snowmen make a very happy Christmas cake, suitable for all ages. The quick and simple way of doing the lettering is very effective, and a rice paper book completes the scene.

Rice paper is edible and can be purchased at cake decorating shops. It is generally white, although colours are available, and it is sold in sheets measuring approximately 18cm x 28cm (7″ x 11″). The paper is transparent and has a different texture on each side, one rough and one smooth.

To transfer designs onto rice paper, place the paper smooth side up over the drawing and trace with a coloured food pen.

Food pens can also be used to colour in the drawing. Alternatively, clear piping gel can be used by painting a thin coat over the surface of the rice paper and colouring with either paste or liquid colours. If using coloured piping gel, cut out the design leaving a tab to transport it, but remember to cut this off before applying to the cake.

No special equipment is needed when using rice paper. It can be cut with ordinary scissors, or a craft knife.

To 'glue' rice paper together, moisten slightly with a paintbrush dampened with water. Only use piping gel when fixing rice paper to a cake.

Keep rice paper well clear of any water — one drop will make a hole.

Side Template
Attach flaps to side of cake with piping gel.

Flat Template
To be placed on cake with piping gel.

Top of Cake Template

1 Cover an oval petal-shaped cake with sugarpaste. Pipe shells of royal icing around the base (No. 1) and attach a ribbon.

2 SIDE DECORATION: Place the rice paper, smooth side up, over the tree design. Using food pens, trace 8 trees onto the paper, 2 with side flaps, before cutting out.

3 TOP DECORATION: Make in the same way as step *2* and fix to the cake-top with piping gel. Fix the side decoration in the same way, attaching 2 of the trees by flaps.

This jolly, festive cake can be made by any member of the family. Children will have great fun decorating their own Christmas cake. All that is needed is a pair of scissors and some rice paper.

Bas-Relief Choirboy

TRACING

Trace the design onto tracing or greaseproof paper. Turn the paper over and go over the lines with a non-toxic pastel pencil or sugarcraft pen. Turn over the paper again and place onto the prepared surface. Trace again following the outline.

Red

Red

White

Red

Black

1 PLAQUE TRACING: *Alternatively, mark the outline of the design either by pricking through with a hat pin, or scratching along the surface with a stylus.*

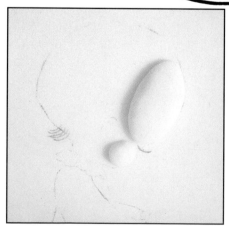

2 *Follow dotted lines on design and fix pieces with rose water.* **Cheek** *Smooth out edges of a small ball of sugarpaste.* **Forehead** *Use tapered roll. Paint hair strands and lashes.*

3 *Cut out the face shape in flesh-coloured sugarpaste. Gently smooth away the 'cut look' with fingertips. Place on face and smooth down edges.*

4 **Hair** *Cut a hole in a piping bag and pipe hair. Stroke the strands, and shape hair with a damp paintbrush.*

5 **Ear** *Make a ball of flesh coloured sugarpaste. Place into position with a damp brush and indent with a ball tool. Dust ear, neck, forehead and cheek with petal dust.*

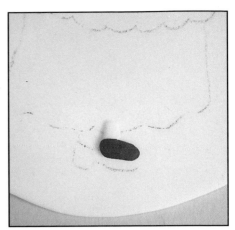

6 **Legs and feet** *Make the leg and rear foot from sugarpaste.*

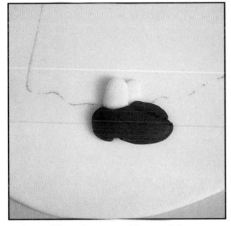

7 *Build up the second leg and foot. Dampen the underside and place into position.*

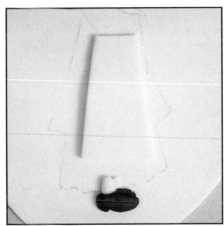

8 *Mould the body from sugarpaste. Leave a space around the outside to 'tuck in' the clothing.*

9 **Cassock** *Roll out a strip of red sugarpaste and frill with a cocktail stick to make folds (see page 46). Dampen the sides and 'tuck in'.*

10 *Cut out pieces of sugarpaste for the top of the cassock, surplice, cuff and hand. Dampen and place into position.*

11 **Main Surplice** *Roll out white sugarpaste and frill edges with a cocktail stick. Dampen edges and tuck around the body. Stroke up folds with a cocktail stick.*

12 *Make an arm and a hand (see page 14). Cut a sleeve from white sugarpaste and frill. Moisten arm with a little rose water, wrap sleeve around and fix into position.*

13 **Collar** Roll out a strip of white sugarpaste and frill with a cocktail stick. Moisten the collar with a little rose water and place into position.

14 Cut out a book from rice paper and place in the choirboy's hands.

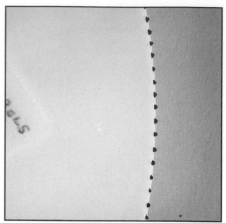

15 Decorate the edge of the plaque with piped dots of royal icing (No.0).

An angelic Choirboy would be a joy to put on a Christmas cake, or a plaque. The plaque could be made up in advance and would sell well at Christmas fetes, etc.

Christmas Table Decoration

1 **FIR CONES:** *Make a cone of brown almond paste and push a cocktail stick up through the base to make a handle.*

2 *Holding the cocktail stick, pipe continuous half-moon shapes of brown royal icing with a petal tube (No. 43). Start at the top of the cone and work downwards.*

3 *Continue piping layers of half-moons around the cone, overlapping and centering each one between the 2 above. Remove the cocktail stick when dry.*

A centre piece such as this will highlight any dinner table at Christmas, and would make an ideal gift for the person 'who has everything'.

Make the candle holder from sugarpaste, indenting the paste with the chosen candle to ensure the correct size. Remove the candle and leave the sugarpaste to dry before assembling the table decoration with a little royal icing.

Silhouette

Silhouettes were the rage of the eighteenth century, but exude a freshness and appeal that belie their ancient heritage. They were sold for decorative purposes, framed or painted directly onto plain walls. They were also used for family likenesses before the advent of photography.

Make family silhouettes by placing a sheet of paper on the wall. Shine a point of light on the subject's profile and trace round the shadow. This can then be reduced on a photocopying machine to the appropriate size.

Suitable designs for silhouettes can be found in newspapers, magazines or on greetings cards.

A graceful Japanese silhouette would be a feature on a cake for any teenager or adult, whether male or female. These silhouettes can be done in any colour, but look dramatic in black.

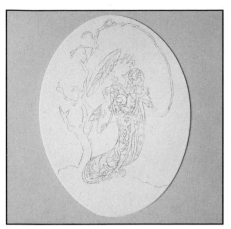

1 Trace the outline onto greaseproof
paper. Place on a plaque of dry
pastillage and mark through with a stylus
pen.

2 Using black food colouring, paint in
the outline with a No. 000 paintbrush.
Paint the wider areas with a No. 2 paintbrush.

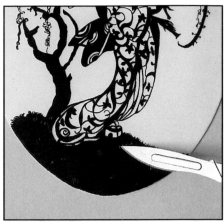

3 When dry, scratch out the fine details
using a sharp pointed scalpel, or craft
knife.

Index